ART DECO
NEW ZEALAND

This book is dedicated to the memory of
Gladys M Goodall QSM, 1908-2015

ART DECO
NEW ZEALAND

AN ILLUSTRATED GUIDE

ILLUSTRATIONS ROSIE LOUISE AND TERRY MOYLE

TERRY MOYLE

Contents

ABOVE: The statue of the explorer Kupe at the Centennial Exhibition of New Zealand, Rongotai Wellington 1939.

NEW ZEALAND

○ Art Deco Towns and Cities

NORTH ISLAND

SOUTH ISLAND

Three Kings Islands
North Cape
CAPE REINGA
Kaitaia
NORTHLAND
Bay of Islands
Kawakawa
WHANGAREI
Dargaville
Wellsford
Warkworth
Great Barrier Island
Kaipara Harbour
Helensville
Hauraki Gulf
AUCKLAND
Thames
Huntly
Paeroa
HAMILTON
TAURANGA
East Cape
Raglan
Bay of Plenty
Cambridge
Te Awamutu
Whakatane
Ruatoria
Lake Rotorua
WAIKATO
ROTORUA
Otorohanga
BAY OF PLENTY
GISBORNE
Taumarunui
Taupo
NEW PLYMOUTH
Lake Taupo
GISBORNE
Mt. Taranaki
Mt. Ruapehu
TARANAKI
MANAWATU-WANGANUI
Hawkes Bay
HAWKES BAY
NAPIER
HASTINGS
WHANGANUI
Waipukurau
PALMERSTON
Dannevirke
NELSON
NORTH
Pahiatua
Golden Bay
Masterton
Tasman Bay
Upper Hutt
NELSON
Picton
Petone
Westport
Blenheim
WELLINGTON
TASMAN
MARLBOROUGH
Cook Strait
Greymouth
Hokitika
WEST COAST
Mt. Cook
CHRISTCHURCH
Lake Pukaki
Banks Peninsula
Ashburton
CANTERBURY
Timaru
Lake Wanaka
Wanaka
Oamaru
Lake Wakatipu
Queenstown
OTAGO
Lake Te Anau
Otago Peninsula
SOUTHLAND
DUNEDIN
Invercargill
Gore
Foveaux Strait
Stewart Island

Illustration for Art Deco New Zealand

Preface

A number of years ago I was talking to Robert McGregor of Napier's Art Deco Trust and we discussed how useful a guide to Art Deco in New Zealand would be. Napier by that stage had been well documented but there was less attention on Art Deco buildings existing outside the Hawke's Bay.

Later I embarked on a two-year Google Earth journey of the streets of the towns and cities of New Zealand. This provided a way of researching the subject previously unavailable. The purpose was to research where one might find art deco buildings. The idea of Art Deco New Zealand as a useful book title developed as the project provided an opportunity to gain a national perspective on Art Deco as well as its presence in individual towns.

As a guide, there is the issue of what you include. The focus is on town centres and noteworthy buildings. As it is understood, Architecture, doesn't always sit comfortably with some of the modest buildings, so Art Deco built heritage is probably a more inclusive terml. As this is intended as a book for a general audience and the visitor, the architectural terms are kept to a minimum.

The definition of Art Deco, with its various design styles and people's different notions on what it is, has become largely associated with the 1920s and 1930s. In real life design styles do not suddenly cease and the buildings considered here lie between the mid-1920s and mid-1950s. The term 'Art Deco' is used here broadly and for the sake of simplicity.

Art Deco houses or Spanish style bungalows became popular in New Zealand in the 1930s and are an essential part of many New Zealander's identification with the style. Domestic Art Deco is not addressed in this book for privacy issues among other reasons. It remains a worthy subject of another book with a different approach. For similar reasons residential architecture and flats are also not considered, nor are schools and hospitals.

It is emphasised that most buildings depicted in this book are not accessible to the public and are private property. Private property rights must be respected.

In many towns and cities there are only a handful of Art Deco commercial buildings that merit interest and sometimes less. The city of Oamaru possesses a most intact and stunningly beautiful Victorian precinct as well as a modern-style public toilet. While this facility may involve an essential visit you wouldn't visit Oamaru for its loo. Given the period of Taupo's construction you are unlikely to encounter Art Deco. There are a few shop façades from the 1930s but Taupo is about wonderful landscapes.

Art Deco was found in places you would not expect. For example the heavily Moderne-style garage in the settlement of Ruatoria on New Zealand's East Coast or the dramatic, two-storey cinema in the far north town of Kawakawa. These buildings are not exactly opera houses in the Amazon jungle but they brought the modern and a sense of the new world and New Zealand's place in that world, to the smallest country town.

Attention is given to groups of Art Deco buildings in streets or towns, rather than individual buildings and I apologise in advance for legitimate candidates that have not been noted. Other built heritage such as monuments, clocks and bridges are not focussed on but mentioned in context.

The level of documentation of the history of these buildings varies immensely within the record keeping of New Zealand's District Councils and other institutions in New Zealand. This means that there are many instances where the construction dates are unknown. With demolished buildings and modified buildings often there are merely a few images and often none whatsoever. The project has involved working with a variety of visual material, including heritage photographs, contemporary images and in particular, illustration.

With over fifty original illustrations, Art Deco New Zealand is one of the most comprehensively illustrated books on New Zealand townscapes ever published. The art represents years of art connected with Art Deco and heritage. The precise vector illustration brings back to life the life and times of Art Deco buildings that have been changed or demolished. The illustration process provides a compelling and evocative way of investigating and then sharing built heritage.

Book creating has always an aspect of exploration and the opportunity to identify where Art Deco can be found in New Zealand led to some interesting discoveries. The former Central Methodist Church in Invercargill 1936 probably represents New Zealand's best example of an 'Art Deco' church and the former Rodney Motors building in Warkworth one of a handful of surviving Streamline Moderne garages in New Zealand. Napier and Hastings are reconsidered. Further afield significant groups of intact Art Deco buildings and semi-precincts are found in New Plymouth, Kaitaia, Te Awamutu, Whakatane, Pahiatua, Petone, Wellington, Nelson, Greymouth, Ranfurly and Gore.

Bringing this art together and working with the images provided by such talented New Zealand photographers, Art Deco and architectural historians has been a privilege. It importantly gives attention to the beauty and character of New Zealand's unique mid-twentieth century built heritage.

Terry Moyle

Introduction

Modern Times

The term 'Art Deco' was largely unheard of in the 1930s. The designing of 'Modern' buildings was the architectural mantra of the time. This was all very well but private investment in commercial building had declined with the Great Depression in 1930.

At the same period as the challenging economics New Zealand society was acutely aware that they were living in modern times, with an unprecedented period of technological change occurring in the world around the island nation. It was a world that was suddenly closer. The 1930s were full of the exploits of feats of long distance flying. Aviators like New Zealander Jean Batten represented New Zealand's stake in this phenomenon; they publicised not only themselves but the prevailing ideas of progress and potential.

In the first years of the Depression, New Zealand exports fell by 45% in two years with unemployment estimated at around 70,000. For New Zealand, the voting in of the first Labour Government in 1935, headed by social reformist, Michael Joseph Savage, was a pivotal moment in New Zealand history. By late 1935 the improving prices for exports meant that the wide-ranging social reforms proposed could be made without threatening the economy. The introduction of a large public works programme would directly lead to construction programmes and numerous modern buildings. In 1936 John A Lee would head up the newly established Department of Housing. The 'State House' building program would see tens of thousands of new homes constructed throughout New Zealand.

The 1935-1949 Labour government transformed the nation. It introduced compulsory trade unionism, sustenance payment rather than relief work. A Factories Act amendment introduced a 40-hour, five-day working week with eight public holidays. A National Employment Service was introduced in 1946 to promote and maintain employment. As well, a large public works programme was introduced 1946 to provide needed employment. The zeal for reform in the years leading up to New Zealand's Centennial added greatly to the idea of a new era. At the Berlin Olympics in 1936, Jack Lovelock had captured the New Zealand imagination by winning the 1500 meters gold medal and setting a new world record.

In 1939 The *New Zealand Listener* was first published; a significant milestone in New Zealand media and social history.

In 1939 TEAL commenced flights between Australia and New Zealand. Tasman Empire Airways Flying Boats represented a triumph of the machine age and for the first time air travel between New Zealand and the rest of the world was a reality. Motor vehicles, and commercial aircraft in particular, were easy to understand manifestations of mechanical progress. Radio Broadcasting had been established and 1940 saw the formation of the New Zealand Symphony Orchestra.

The country had optimistically looked forward to celebrating the milestone of 100 years in 1940.

New Zealander's relationship with Art Deco styling and building construction coincided with the Nation's Centennial. The Great Depression had seen the emergence of a Government that introduced the benefits to its citizens at an unprecedented level. There were numerous projects created to provide employment including the construction of picture theatres in towns throughout New Zealand, many of which were identified accordingly as 'State' picture theatres.

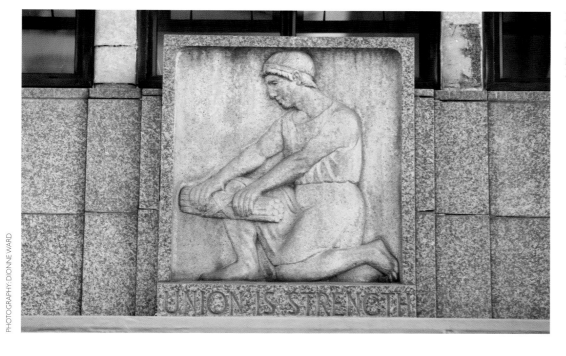

LEFT: This carved stone bas relief with the line 'UNION IS STRENGTH" sits above the impressive entrance to the Wellington's MLC Building in the CBD.

The Modern had already become evident in many New Zealand towns and cities.

Along with a sense of the country being reinvigorated and the idea of the nation's coming of age (1940 being one hundred years since the signing of the Treaty of Waitangi) was the expression of identity and progress through the construction of modern buildings and often a modern clock in the centre of town.

In 1931 New Zealand's population was estimated at 1,522,800. By 1940 the population was 1,633,600 (with an astounding 2.6 million visitors to the Centennial Exhibition).

Throughout the 20th century the shift from rural areas to urban areas increased. In 1940 the urban population was over 65% but by the end of the century this had increased to approximately 85%. Although Auckland was still the region with the largest population, it had yet to exhibit the spectacular growth that by 2016 would see approximately one third of the country's population resident in the region.

The distribution (estimated) of New Zealand population in April 1939 was quite different. Auckland City (excluding the associated boroughs) had a population of 106,000, with boroughs making up 221,500. Wellington City (excluding the associated boroughs) had 119,000, and with boroughs claimed 157,900 resident. Christchurch boroughs had an estimated 135,400 and Dunedin 82,800. Hamilton Borough 20,800, Gisborne 16,300, Napier 19,400, Hastings 18,900, New Plymouth 19,300, Whanganui City, 26,100, Palmerston North City 25,300, Nelson 14,000, Timaru 19,300 and Invercargill City 26,500.

Tauranga 3,860 and Waihi 4010. Pahiatua recorded 2,880 and Gore 4,770.[2] The smaller, more homogenous, more evenly distributed population of Auckland helps explain the presence of apparently major buildings in small towns and the relative small number of Art Deco buildings in centres that grew exponentially with post-Second World War urbanisation.

New Zealand Art Deco buildings are, with a few exceptions, not flamboyant or as decorated as those designed in Australia and in particular, the United States. Function and purpose are apparent in the vast majority. Even the decorated former Auckland Electric Power Board Building (1929) in Queen Street, adopted a style complete with decoration to practically promote the virtues of the reliable supply of electric power.

In 1929 the first hydro electricity in New Zealand was generated with the commissioning of the Arapuni Hydro Dam. New Zealanders rightly felt that they were living in modern times. Then there was the share market crash in 1929 and the worldwide Depression. New Zealand experienced upheaval as the economy faltered. Nor were upheavals restricted to the stock exchange.

In The 1929 Murchison earthquake in the South Island caused considerable damage to the town of Westport and Nelson. In Westport the post office tower collapsed and other brick buildings were damaged. The 1929 earthquake took 17 lives. The destruction was not on the scale of Napier but did later result in the construction of one of New Zealand's finest Art Deco buildings in Westport.

The 1931 Hawke's Bay earthquake saw destruction and associated reconstruction on a scale not seen before. The loss of nearly the entirety of Napier's business district meant that a coordinated approach to design could be adopted in the rebuilding of the town. This coordination, and the undergrounding of electricity and telephone services, meant the result was a very modern precinct that made use of a range of Art Deco styles with considerable harmony between the buildings. This consistency in design, also evident in Hastings, contributes to the slightly film-set quality of our retrospective experience. The impression that was created and desired was one of good taste. Napier subsequently basked in its modernity as the newest city in New Zealand.

Another destructive earthquake, the Pahiatua earthquake, occurred on March 5, 1934. Hawke's Bay, already recovering from the 1931 earthquake experienced damage as did Wairarapa and Wellington. The town of

Pahiatua was extensively damaged. The associated reconstruction resulted in a collection of small-scale 1930s commercial buildings. While far more modest than Napier, Hastings or even Westport, Pahiatua small-town built-heritage owes as much to 1930s earthquakes as the better-known northern towns.

On February 22, 2011 Christchurch, New Zealand's third largest city, was severely damaged by a magnitude 6.3 earthquake. The earthquake killed 185 people and caused thousands of injuries.

Many heritage buildings were irreparably damaged and the earthquake saw the loss of the city's former Art Deco theatres. It represented the greatest loss of Art Deco architecture in a single event to occur in New Zealand. It also occurred at a time of greater consciousness and appreciation of New Zealand's Art Deco buildings than ever before.

The catastrophe highlights the precariousness of New Zealand's built heritage in a country that experiences frequent earthquakes and the ambivalent role these have played in both the construction of Art Deco buildings and their destruction. Fires also have played their part and have also led to the construction of hotels, council chambers and other commercial buildings. Earthquakes also caused a shift in the standards used in constructing buildings and New Zealand multi storey buildings were constructed in reinforced concrete. New Zealand in the 1930s became regarded internationally as having some expertise in constructing earthquake resistant structures.

The Post Office – the presence of the State

After the Labour Government of 1935 came to power with its wide-ranging reforms, the State appeared to have become omniscient in the matters of the nation. Its physical presence came in the form of new buildings, particularly the post office. At the time of the opening of Hamilton's new chief Post Office, the Postmaster General Patrick C Webb MP was proclaiming the construction of three new post offices (Hamilton, Whanganui, Invercargill) in the same year as memorials to New Zealand's centennial. At the outbreak of war Mr Webb said that the Government had planned to build a 100 new post offices, all of which were needed.[3]

Until the 1980s the true commercial centre of the New Zealand town was the post office. The post office was also a significant employer. In Pahiatua, for example, the mid-1930s post office had over 20 employees serving a population of around 3000.

An unprecedented construction period of post offices was undertaken during the 1930s and 1940s. The Government architect, John T Mair (1876-1959) designed many of these buildings or at least oversaw their design. John Mair was appointed Government architect in 1923. During the Depression, Mair ensured that local architects and builders in towns outside Wellington were given work on government construction work. He designed the pavilion for Rotorua's Blue Baths (1936) and Classical courthouses in Hamilton (1931) and Blenheim (1939).

The typically Stripped Classical post office design communicated a desirable impression of authority while the style complemented the older buildings in its proximity.

The buildings frequently introduced decorative elements to varying degrees and these were sometimes used to identify the place in which the post office building was erected. Local materials were also used in construction. The use of Waikato Hinuera stone in the building of the chief Post Office in Hamilton for example.

The rate of building was feverish and during the period 1930 to 1935 an estimated 17 post offices were constructed. In the next five years, after the Labour Government assumed power, this more than doubled, with substantial post offices being built in Dunedin, Hamilton, Whanganui, Lower Hutt, Tauranga, Dunedin and Invercargill.

As well as mail and freight, the post office provided banking facilities, licensing, telegram and telephone services. While the predominantly Stripped Classical Art Deco style used may appear conservative when seen against later designs, they still represented a shift in the type of building in many New Zealand towns. The post office construction was a vital part of a national building programme that is unlikely to be repeated.

The Pictures and the 'Talkies'

The 1930s had seen the introduction of sound, and cinemas in New Zealand were built to take advantage of this technology. Cinemas and theatres in New Zealand, as elsewhere, gave the architect (budget permitting), a chance to explore more creative and exotic structures. Theatres had always been an excuse for the architect to indulge in more fanciful design, particularly in the interior of the buildings. The eclectic nature of Art Deco saw uninhibited borrowing from other cultures and the interior decorations of theatres would frequently have Egyptian, South American and Indian elements to add more exoticism to the theatre experience.

In the Depression years (1929-1935) many picture theatres were constructed around the country under an incentive scheme offered by the government which subsidized theatre construction on a pound for pound basis. Accordingly such theatres were known as 'State' theatres.

In New Zealand small towns the theatre was frequently the most Art Deco building in the townscape with its architecture and films bringing the modern world to rural New Zealand.

Hotels and Pubs

Slightly less important than the post office in the 1930s and, at least as important as the theatre was the town hotel or hotels. Historically in towns these were large two-storeyed wooden buildings offering accommodation, dining and bar facilities. In the mid-1930s hotels were reconstructed or built along clean modern lines and reinforced concrete. A repeated type was a ferro-concrete building where the curved elements so characteristic of Streamline Moderne served their purpose on corner building sites.

There was modernising of existing hotels, which usually involved removal of detail considered extraneous and replastering a modern façade.

While new hotels were still being constructed often a hotel would be redesigned with ferro-concrete façade that was modern in appearance. In rural locations the Art Deco house design was adpated and made larger in scale for various commercial buildings.

Institutional Art Deco Buildings

The Government or large financially secure companies instigated most of the larger scale projects in New Zealand in the 1930s. These companies largely pursued a house-style in the design of their buildings. The size and scale of the building was often in proportion to the significance and size of the town.

Bank Buildings

Built throughout the 1930s, these National Bank buildings were invariably Stripped Classical in style with decorative patterns. Bank of New Zealand premises range from Classical to Stripped Classical, before then, in the late 1930s and 1940s, adopting more modern styles. The bank persisted with decoration on exteriors into the 1950s.

T&G Buildings

These tall buildings with an inevitable ziggu-

LEFT: Stripped Classical Tauranga Post Office, circa 1940s.

BELOW: The exuberant Art Deco New Zealand Pavilion designed by Edmund Anscombe, and in the background the Australian Pavilion, from the Centennial Exhibition of New Zealand, Rongotai Wellington 1939.

rat tower and 'house style' were constructed in Auckland, Hamilton, Napier, Palmerston North, Wellington and Christchurch. With numerous buildings in Australia, the Temperance and General Mutual Assurance Life Society (T&G) dated from 1876 and originated in Victoria. During the 1920s and 1930s the T&G constructed many of these white-painted imposing buildings in Australia and New Zealand. Their height and appearance provided an impression of progress and modernity that was aspired to at the time.

CML Buildings

The Colonial Mutual Life Assurance Society Ltd (CML) was another Australian company that erected distinctive buildings during the 1930s. The multi-storeyed buildings graced the skylines of Australian and New Zealand towns and cities.

MLC Buildings

Although constructed into the 1950s, the Mutual Life & Citizens Assurance Company Limited (MLC) buildings with their clock towers and detailing owe more to the 1930s. Wellington, Auckland and Hamilton possess MLC buildings.

The 1940 Centennial Exhibition

In New Zealand the opening of the first hydroelectric dam at Arapuni in 1929 had provided not only a reliable supply for a rapidly expanding Auckland but brought a heightened sense of the world-changing qualities of technology.

The New Zealand Centennial Exhibition Company, all comprised of Directors from Wellington, first met in 1936. The Directors issued share certificates that were picked up by local government, including Wellington City Council, Auckland, Eastbourne, Fielding, Lower Hutt, Masterton, Napier, Palmerston North, Petone, Whanganui city and borough councils and the Manawatu County Council.

Transport companies and banks also acquired shares. Major shareholders include well-known New Zealand companies.

Architect Edmund Anscombes' experience with the Dunedin NZ and South Seas International Exhibition of 1925-26 had been ambivalent to say the least. He had clashed with the committee and, at the end of the arrangement, published a document (at his own expense) condemning the way in which the exhibition had been run. The 1940 exhibition was opened on November 8, 1939. The event attracted 20,000 people to the opening but the mood was sobered by the declaration of war against Germany a month earlier. Already men were volunteering for the services.

If Stripped Classical style had been in favour in the thirties by both State and banking institutions, the 1940 Centennial exhibition was celebrated in an Art Deco Style that was exuberantly modern. The exhibition featured an impressive Art Deco tower decorated with a bas-relief frieze by artist Alison Duff that included depictions of New Zealand's progress with images of motor vehicles and tractors. The centrepiece was a large reflective pond with a statue of Polynesian explorer Kupe and his companions catching first sight of Aotearoa.

The exhibition hall walls, otherwise plain, had their uniformity augmented by Streamline Moderne motifs and lines. While it is being generous to describe the buildings, which were temporary and constructed using timber and asbestos covering, as the most extensive manifestation of 'Streamline Moderne in the world,' the designs of the Exhibition communicated progress to the many visitors.[1]

And there were many visitors. The phenomenal attendance figures give an idea of the impact the Exhibition had. There were 2.6 million visitors and at the time the country's population was only 1.5 million. The majority of visitors were not attending to admire the efforts of the architect and the accounts of state progress but to enjoy the entertainments offered by 'Playland'. Playland was a theme park offering rides on the Octopus and the Cyclone, and the architecture that was most enthused about was the Crazy House; an entertainment of collapsing floors, mazes and mirrors.

While Edmund Anscombe's creations where the epitome of the contemporary, Streamline Moderne was rarely adopted for commercial buildings in New Zealand partly because it was a style, with rounded corners, that was very site specific. More fundamentally the increased popularity and better economics associated with the International style, and its emphasis on function quickly established itself as the favoured construction style for the remainder of the 20th century.

For commercial buildings, Streamline Moderne was often adopted when there was a corner site to be considered and many hotels from the late 1930s to the early 1950s were built or refurbished accordingly. Decoration with such buildings was reduced to simple bas-relief parallel lines. These were either quite short and located on the curved corners of a building or at the ends of the façade. There were variations including the circles with three short parallel horizontal lines on either side. The façades also favoured larger raised letters for the name of the building with simple sans-serif fonts favoured over the more artful style of the early to mid 1930s. The reduction of decoration to these simple elements made it easier for modest shop fronts to look contemporary with minimal expense or effort.

While Moderne style building was modestly represented in New Zealand commercial buildings, the style suited residential dwellings that were unencumbered by adjacent buildings. The Spanish bungalow design for houses became very popular, while Spanish Mission Style elements and a concrete finish with rounded corners, were typical of

their construction. Peter Shaw uses the term 'Spanish Deco' which combined a Streamlined Moderne house with the decorative details common to Spanish Mission. Now these buildings are more commonly called Art Deco houses, with designs with varying degrees of Streamlined Moderne qualities or Spanish elements, depending on the preferences of the architect.

Streamline Moderne was adopted by the motor industry for some of its garages. The post-war era meant a boom in motor vehicle ownership as well as a lessening of restrictions on motor fuels. The style, which always had a physical association with the design and performance of aircraft, motor vehicles and locomotives of the 1930s, was represented in the style of new garages and service stations in the post-war era. The most notable example in the New Zealand Road Services terminal in Dunedin, the centre for bus and omnibus transport in that city. A number of service stations, often combined with car dealerships, used the style in both the building and the canopies that were constructed over the petrol bowsers. The new stations were conspicuously different to pre-war facilities that were generally made from red brick complemented by illuminated signage. Notable examples survive in the former Latty's garage in Gore that still function as a garage, although the petrol bowsers have long gone. In Napier a Streamline garage was constructed in 1938 and operated by the Hawke's Bay Farmers, although the building itself has in later years been considerably modified. Similarly in Warkworth, the former Rodney Motors building was designed in a Streamline Moderne style, with some surviving Art Deco decoration still clearly visible.

A New Zealand Art Deco?
If there is an Art Deco style that can make any claim to be a national style, then it may be seen in the Stripped Classical post offices and public buildings that provided gov-

RIGHT: For many small Art Deco commercial buildings in New Zealand modernity was all about the typeface, cheap building materials, and the simple shape of the building. Newton King Ltd, an old produce store in Te Kuiti epitomies this.

PHOTOGRAPHY: TERRY MOYLE

ernment services constructed in the 1930s. Most of these were designed either by or under the direction of John T Mair.

1940 was to be the zenith of Art Deco in New Zealand. New buildings had appeared, adorned with Māori motif. Streamlined buildings at the New Zealand Pavilion reached for the stars. Then in September 1939, the war with Germany and that underlying sense of dread by those New Zealander's for whom the horrors of the First World War were still fresh in their memories. Then in the following year Michael Joseph Savage, the Prime Minister of New Zealand dies on March 27. In 1941 John Mair, who had overseen so many projects in New Zealand and designed so many public buildings, retired from his position as Government architect.

Building construction in 1930s and 1940s New Zealand was both limited by the economics of Depression and correspondingly stimulated by Government investment in building. New Zealand possesses a relatively small number of substantial Art Deco buildings, and although the Art Deco precinct of Napier is intact and designed in a coordinated manner, the buildings are generally single or two-storeyed. This was also a reflection of the fact that the Hawke's Bay region was subject to frequent earthquakes.

Institutional investment in building by the National Bank of New Zealand in particular, contributed much to the Stripped Classical style that found favour in New Zealand towns. More typically however, the owners of commercial premises adopted the decorations and style of Art Deco on the façades of their buildings, while the rest of the structure, with the exception of some Moderne leadlight glass, was purely functional. This modest and functional approach to Art Deco reflected the desire of businesses to be seen as progressive while involving minimal expense.

PHOTOGRAPHY: PETRA ZOE, TERRY MOYLE

LEFT: ASB Bank in Napier noted for it's elaborate Māori decoration on a otherwise Stripped Classical building.

BELOW: Carved Māori koruru heads on the old Rotorua Police Station.

The designing of something along 'modern-lines' frequently involved the use of stepped parapets and façades. Layered fin pilasters and simple squares announced the contemporaneousness of the building, whether a McKenzie's store in Petone or a picture theatre in Kawakawa, Northland, both built in 1937.

The style of lettering adopted on these façades and halls and the minimal decoration in bas-relief were readily used by the designers of both large and small commercial buildings throughout New Zealand. The simplicity of the Modern styles and the use of Art Deco typefaces represented an inexpensive but effective way to accent an otherwise plain structure.

New Zealand retail chains like Farmers Trading Co. and McKenzies refurbished their existing shops to a Moderne appearance. Art Deco was used in the construction of police stations, banks, hotels, theatres, and all manner of retail business. It was used in the design of public toilets, airport buildings, service stations, dentists, town clocks, butchers and drapers.

Despite Māori having a wealth of decorative elements and a decorative tradition, Art Deco architecture was slow to borrow Māori motif. Art Deco styling had already opened the way for the use of indigenous Māori motif in New Zealand buildings. The Bank of New Zealand in Napier feature extensive Māori inspired decoration on both exterior and interior. The Police Stations in Rotorua and Palmerston North also borrowed motif for the decoration of buildings. The Chief Post Office in Whanganui possesses the most assertive presence of; Māoriness'; the koruru heads were worked into the characteristically Stripped Classical design of the building by the architect. That, with the exception of Napier, most of these buildings were constructed around the Centennial reflected

an emerging awareness of Māori identity in the make-up of New Zealand.

Tretheway's sculpture of Kupe and the construction of a Māori Court at the 1940 exhibition were championed by Sir Apirana Ngata. Ngata had driven the establishment of the School of Māori Arts and Crafts in Rotorua in 1927. This facility was at the forefront of marae redevelopment in the North Island.

The Māori Court at the Centennial Exhibition was designed and carved under Ngata's supervision and the master carver was Pine Taiapa. The large building was intended to showcase an egalitarian progressive society, however government policies of the time were essentially assimilative which was counter to the desire and need for Māori individuality, which leading to a loss of identity. Loss of identity occurred in a figurative sense. The palm frond motifs and zigzag decoration, while identified as derived from the Māori decorative canon, owe their existence to Mayan and other decorative traditions that were internationally represented in Art Deco buildings'. The similarities were sufficient for the associations to be perfectly acceptable. The actual number of buildings of the period using Māori motif was in fact small and all examples can be considered rare. The all-purpose assimilative Stripped Classical style was the most common building type used. The 1936 East Coast Commission building in Gisborne was an exception, where the fusing of the Streamlined Moderne style and the verticality of traditional Māori carving pointed to an entirely different and unexplored direction.

Whatever one's views of appropriation of Māori motif, the end of the era of decorative Art Deco buildings, leaves us considering what more could have been developed from such a rich and indigenous decorative tradition.

Social Change from the 1980s

Changes in technology and a retreat from government ownership in the mid-1980s affected the institutions once regarded as the centres of small town life. New Zealand postal service, which once combined banking, telephone and postal services, was deconstructed into separate commercial entities. The grand buildings of the 1930s and 1940s were no longer needed. The movie theatres that had been built to accommodate the 'talkies' and marked the end of the silent film era, found themselves competing with television and videos. The move towards home entertainment, first through videos, then through Digital Video Disks (DVDs) and finally through the availability of films via the Internet, irrevocably changed the role of picture theatres.

The other focus of town life, the

ABOVE: Aerial view of Napier from the Marine Parade with the former T&G Building in the foreground.

ABOVE: The Masonic Hotel (1932-33) was a place for Napier social functions as well as catering to the many guests. It was Napier's largest hotel and regarded as its finest. Large Art Deco-styled lounges with comfortable arm chairs offered those staying, according to the advertising of the era, 'amenities hitherto unknown to hotel life in Napier.' One of the entrances features an extensive glass leadlight awning.

ABOVE: The Government Building (1938) reflects the Stripped Classical style favoured by the Government architect JT Mair. Napier's Hill is a backdrop to this. It is notable being the only building in Napier of the period to feature stone cladding. The iconic lamp and twin lamps on the entrance reflect the favouring of decorative exterior lighting on government buildings. The car is a Morris 10/4 from 1936.

ABOVE: A rare example of Stream-line Moderne style was the original Hawke's Bay Farmer's Co-op garage located at 97 Dalton Street. It was designed by EA Williams of Napier. Now operating as a retail store, the original façade is believed to be intact under the steel cladding.

of skilled planning and of very fine cultural taste.' [2]

The Marine Parade would continue to be developed and added to over the years. The Tom Parker Fountain with it's coloured illumination at night, mini golf range, and in later years the marine life facility, and children playgrounds. Such development reflects the ongoing importance of the gardens to Napier. A former Mayor's vision of a 'noble promenade' would be realised in a sea-front recreational amenity that embodies the spirit and activities indelibly associated with the Art Deco era.

The Art Deco precinct of Napier is built around Tennyson and Emerson Streets, and includes the Marine Parade to the east and to Clive Square located to the west. The precinct includes a range of styles that were in favour at the time and include Spanish Mission, Prairie School, Stripped Classical and Moderne. Despite the range of styles, the consistency in the scale of the buildings and the materials used have ensured the precinct presents as harmonious.

Hurst's Building (1932) at 125 Emerson Street, is a two-storey reinforced concrete structure that served as a photography shop and studio. With its richly decorated parapet it was possibly the first Art Deco building to be constructed in the Napier town centre following the 1931 earthquake.

ABOVE & RIGHT: Formerly known as the Bank of New Zealand, now the ASB Bank, this building is a unique example of Stripped Classical decorated with Māori patterns.

BELOW: The decoration continues inside with the grand coffered ceiling bordered by Māori rafter designs.

The Emerson Building at 93 Emerson Street (dated 1931 on the building façade but completed in 1932) is a Spanish Mission design.

The iconic T&G Building at 1 Emerson Street was designed by Wellington architects, Atkin and Mitchell, and was completed 1935-1936. The three-storey reinforced concrete building featured a dome of unpainted copper which oxidised to a green colour. The building was constructed by Napier building contractor, WM Angus.

The Hawke's Bay Museum was designed by Wright and Louis Hay and was built in 1936 and 1937. In 2013 a second wing was added as part of the refurbishment.

Parker's Chambers is a Louis Hay design. The red brick of the building is used as a decorative veneer over the concrete structure underneath.

The massive hill behind Napier and the town's dramatic location in Hawke's Bay embody the non-architectural aspects of New Zealand Art Deco. The country's fabulous scenery and characteristic clear light, superbly complement Art Deco buildings,

CLOCK-WISE FROM TOP LEFT: Rose motifs carved into the spandrel panels under the windows on the exterior walls; carved Tudor roses that form the ends of an Art Nouveau style sunburst above the entrance; grapes, vines and leaves decorate either side of the front entrance; lavishly decorated interior with roses in leadlight and on the plaster ceiling and walls. Imported marble was used for the wainscot, and the door hardware was in bronze.

particularly those constructed in the Spanish Mission style. Napier enjoys an international reputation and role in the identity of Art Deco, and arguably influenced the style of other towns. In the late 1930s, with the development of the Bay of Plenty town of Whakatane, it is impossible to discount the influence of Napier.

One of the notable aspects of Napier's buildings was the introduction of indigenous decoration in the interior and exteriors of these buildings. The Bank of New Zealand building (1932), designed by Crichton, McKay and Haughton introduced Māori kōwhaiwhai ceiling panels. The Ross and Glendinning building (1932) constructed in the same year incorporates Māori design in its exterior decoration.

By the 1980s, 50 years after the construction, it was suggested that Art Deco had become a local symbol and the image of Napier an important place in the establishment of New Zealand's identity. The idea of the brave rebuild and the spectacular results are compelling in themselves. In a practical sense Napier citizens in the 1980s recognised this and established an Art Deco group to promote a revived interest in Napier's splendid collection of buildings.

In 1987 The Art Deco Trust was legally incorporated. Then in 1992, with support from the Napier City Council, the Trust became a full time entity, with staff and

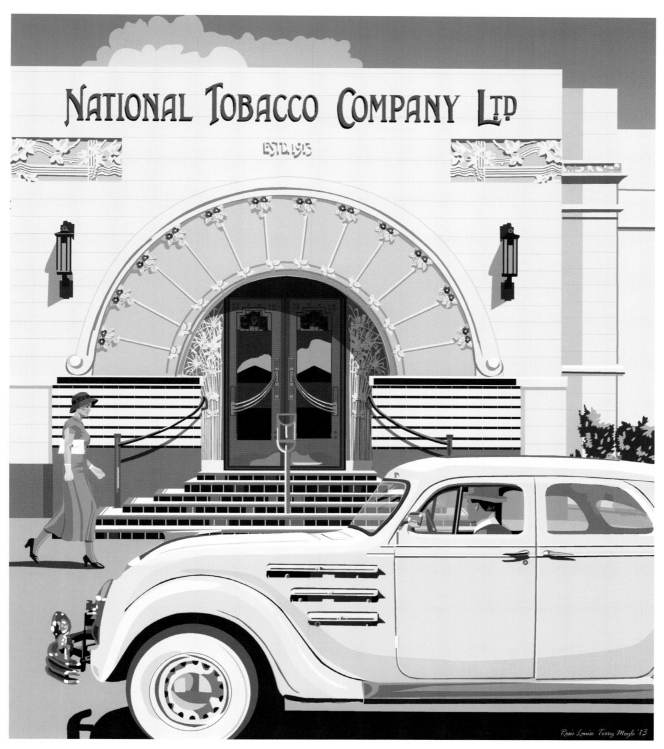

ABOVE: In 1935 the health issues of smoking were not so apparent and contention over tobacco packaging and advertising did not exist. The National Tobacco factory provided a 'Hollywood-like front' complete with floral decoration suggesting sophistication and even health benefits. The entrance lobby was dome-lit with beautiful oak doors and panelling. A writer in 1935 noted 'The factory was a revelation: 'We took the girls at afternoon tea (provided by the management) and the clatter of tongues and ripples of laughter made one think of birds on a summer afternoon.'

NATIONAL LIBRARY FL 16799712

premises. With over a hundred dedicated volunteers, Napier has successfully translated its distinctive architecture into a desirable destination for visitors.

The Trust's role in lobbying for and highlighting Napier's Art Deco built heritage has not only generated much civic pride, but has helped make Napier one of the places to see for people visiting New Zealand. The hosting of Napier's Art Deco Festival sees an annual re-enactment of these earlier times and other events where people and visitors, both from New Zealand and overseas, dress in period style. Vintage vehicles and Art Deco related events draw tens of thousands to the Hawke's Bay, and Napier's Marine Parade.

In a national sense Napier, New Zealand's once 'newest' city has spearheaded Art Deco tourism established around the city's unique and beautiful built heritage. No other New Zealand town has such a concentration of 1930s commercial buildings.

NAPIER ART DECO TRUST

TOP: The Napier State Theatre in the early 1940s. The film showing is *The Little Princess* starring Shirly Temple.

ABOVE: Former Hildebrandt's building, designed by architect JA Louis Hay in 1933.

CLOCK-WISE FROM TOP: A postcard of the Hawke's Bay Museum from 1937; detail on the two-storeyed Hurst building, 125 Emerson Street, designed by Finch & Westerholm, Napier; New Zealand Māori pattern was used on the former Ross & Glendining Ltd (Antiques Centre), 65 Tennyson Street designed in 1932 by Napier architect, EA Williams. The different indigenous designs are placed adjacent so the similarities and differences in form can be appreciated; Mayan influenced decorative detail on the former Bank of New South Wales (Crombe Lockwood building), in 32 Hastings Street. It was designed in 1933, the architects were Chrichton, McKay & Haughton, Wellington.

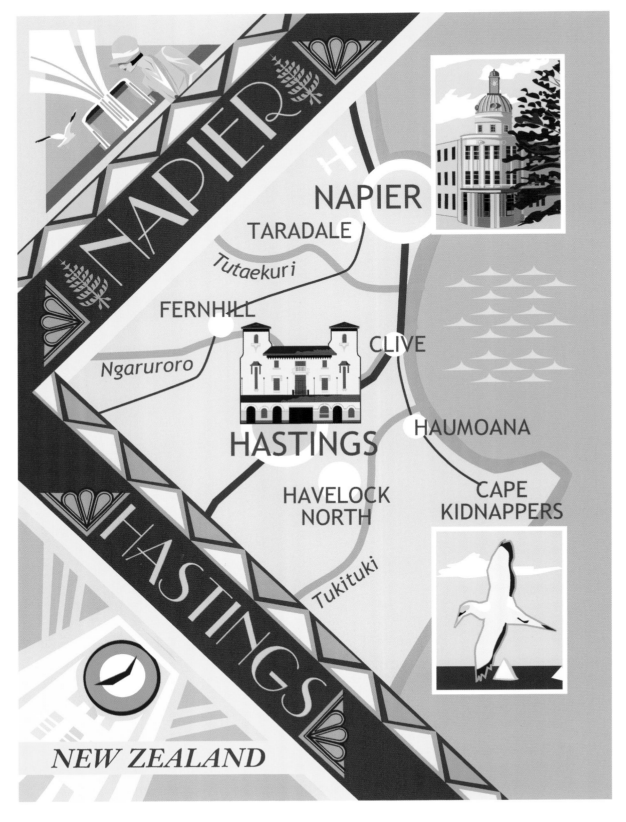

NAPIER

NAPIER

TARADALE

Tutaekuri

FERNHILL

CLIVE

Ngaruroro

HASTINGS

HAUMOANA

HAVELOCK NORTH

CAPE KIDNAPPERS

Tukituki

HASTINGS

NEW ZEALAND

PHOTOGRAPHY: TERRY MOYLE '13

Hastings

The Hawke's Bay town of Hastings had embraced Spanish Mission architecture twenty years prior to the devastating 1931 earthquake. The popular revivalist design style is evident in both private residences and commercial buildings constructed throughout the twentieth century to the present day. The dry climate and long sunshine hours of the region suited this association. The style had become popular internationally arriving in New Zealand in the late 19th century, and early twentieth century. Spanish Mission style, at its minimum combined a plaster finish and tiled roofs, and decorative elements like barley twists. It had been established as Hawke's Bay style by the construction of iconic buildings including the outstanding Hastings' Municipal Theatre designed by architect Henri Eli White in 1912.

The theatre auditorium was notable for it's fine acoustics, and excellent ventila-

ABOVE: Spanish Mission influenced Wesley Methodist Church on Hastings Street was built in early 1932.

ART DECO NEW ZEALAND **37**

ABOVE: Postcard of Heretaunga Street in the 1950s showing the State Theatre on the left and the Westerman's & Co. building on the corner on the right.

tion, as well as uninterrupted sight lines. While the interior of the theatre featured White's favouring of Art Nouveau elements, notably the use of stem-like forms, the exterior of the building was unabashedly decorated with Spanish Mission elements. Tiled roofed towers are located on either end of the front elevation arched windows, doors and a decorative balustrade.

The 1914 Municipal Chambers are attributed to Garnett and feature elements that are in sympathy with the adjacent Municipal Theatre, the Chamber's prominent tower with its tiled roof creating an excellent visual relationship to the theatre's twin towers.

The Methodist Church was rebuilt to

plans drawn up by the firm of Harold Davies and Eric Phillips in 1931-1932. Davies had previously designed the Hastings Baptist Church in 1916. Davies partner was Eric Phillips (1897-1980) and the firm was particularly active in the 1930s in using the Art Deco style in Hastings and the Hawke's Bay. The new Methodist Church was a rare example of an Art Deco style church, although its modern tower was embellished with Spanish Mission qualities.

Synonymous with Spanish Mission architecture, the Hawke's Bay town of Hastings, just 22km south of Napier, had been similarly affected by the 1931 earthquake, although it avoided the fires that wiped out

LEFT: The attractive Westerman's & Co. building on the corner of Russell Street was built by Edmund Ascombe and Associates in 1932, revives the Spanish Mission style with barley twist columns, and terracotta tiles mixed with Classical elements. The State Theatre can be seen in the background.

BELOW: The Hastings Art Deco clock tower was built in 1935.

LEFT: Opposite Westermans on the corner of Heretaunga Street West and Russell Street South is the R & R Building which was designed in 1927 by local archictect Harold Davies. It survived the Napier earthquake unscathed.

PHOTOGRAPHY: TERRY MOYLE '13

ABOVE: Former CML Build-
ing, corner of Russell Street
South and Eastbourne Street.

RIGHT: The Municipal Theatre
built by Henry Eli White was
officially opened in 1915. The
Council Chambers were built in
1917 and designed by architect
Albert Garnett.

the Napier central business district. In Napier 161 perished and in Hastings 93 people lost their lives. With less visible monuments than Napier's Marine Parade, the Methodist church's slightly monumental quality seems entirely appropriate.

The rebuilding of Hastings involved a level of self-interested cooperation. In Napier there was a need to establish a local association of architects. The association included Hastings representatives including the firms of Edmund Anscombe and Associates and Davies Garnett and Phillips.

Davies and Phillips would design the former Dental and Medical Chambers in 1935 and the Heretaunga Building's (1936) which was a rebuild of the original 1922 building that brought the style and material favoured into the design of a prominent commercial building. The 1932 Queens Chambers and the former Commercial Bank of Australia were designed with Stripped Classical detail.

Edmund Anscombe who would later design the modern-looking buildings and layout for the 1940 Centennial Exhibition showed his adeptness with Spanish Mission styling. The Westerman and Co department store in 1932 involved dividing the Russell Street elevation into three sections that used Spanish Mission features. On the shorter elevation he integrated round-headed windows flanked by square-headed ones and on the splayed corner he featured a doorway framed with barley twist half columns and fluted Corinthian pilasters. Spanish Mission buildings exist elsewhere but Anscombe's design reintroduces the qualities of the surviving municipal buildings.

The Hastings Post Office (1932) is designed in the signature, Stripped Classical style of that service. Designed by John T Mair at a cost of £12,022 the building was constructed with reinforced concrete. The design with pilasters topped by an acanthus leaf

ABOVE: The Municipal Theatre designed in Spanish Mission style by architect Henri Eli White in 1912.

RIGHT: The former Commercial Bank of Australia, 2013. The Te Mata Peak is in the background.

BELOW: Karamu Road. The building in the middle of the three is the Hawke's Bay Farmers Meat Co. (1931). The former Karamu Chambers Buildings (1935) are to the right at 124 – 126 Karamu Rd North. Stripped Classical Karamu Chambers were designed by Davies and Phillips.
The building to the left was a business building originally designed by C Tilleard, Natusch and Sons in 1925 for Mr P Cohen.

PHOTOGRAPHY: TERRY MOYLE '13

decoration and some abstract iconic design.

The State Theatre (1934) was designed by Edmund Anscombe and Auckland architectual student Vernon Brown in 1933 in a Stripped Classical style. Central Building (1934) and the Dominion Restaurant (1935) are buildings that are modest in Art Deco presentation but contribute to the townscape.

The Hastings town clock arrived in 1935 and was the result of an architectural competition judged by Davies and Phillips. The resulting clock tower was more in-clined to be modern than Spanish Mission, comprising a vertical reinforced concrete rectangle surmounted by a disc and flagpole. It was designed to house the bells of the post office tower (1909) damaged in the 1931 Hawke's Bay earthquake. Located near the railway lines and across the road from the Westerman and Co building the tower has served Hastings well as a recognizable icon.

The Colonial Mutual Life building (1939) connects with this landmark. Designed by Swan and Lavelle, the building's octagonal and tiled tower was in sympathy with

PHOTOGRAPHY: MERCEDES WAITERE

LEFT: The Arcadia Picture Theatre built in 1919 is a fine example of early Spanish Mission architecture.

BELOW: The Masonic Hotel illustrated as in the early 1950s.

Dannevirke

Dannevirke in the Manawatu region has a fascinating range of built heritage and architecture. These include the very fine Arcadia Picture Theatre (1919) at 84 High Street, one of New Zealand's few surviving theatres from the silent age of film. It was constructed in Spanish Mission style as was the highly visible former Masonic Hotel built on the corner of High Street and Barraud Street. The Masonic was rebuilt after a major fire in 1918, in which twenty-seven shops were destroyed. Originally constructed with a corner tower, the structure was removed following the 1931 Hawke's Bay earthquake and the hotel was remodelled to a more hyrbrid Art Deco appearance. The building forms part of a substantial group of 1920s two-storey buildings in Dannevirke, including the adjacent red brick Masonic Chambers. There is an impressive collection of buildings around the junction of High Street and Gordon Street, including the majestic Classical Bank of New Zealand and former Dannevirke Post Office. From this junction, Gordon Street affords attractive rural views.

Pahiatua

PHOTOGRAPHY: GERRY PARKER

The reconstruction following the Hawke's Bay earthquake resulted in two significant centres of Art Deco buildings in New Zealand. Further south in the Tararua District, the town of Pahiatua was subject to similar upheavals as Napier and Hastings. An earthquake with a magnitude of 7.5 occurred on March 5, 1934 causing severe damage. For the small town this destructive event no doubt contributed to the construction of the 1930s commercial buildings in the town. Although there are buildings of later eras in the main street, and older buildings have undergone modernising, Pahiatua has an enviable collection of small town Art Deco buildings.

The landmark Tui brewery and Tui brew tower (1931), several kilometres to the north of Pahiatua heading south, is a rare surviving example of an industrial building of the period. Until 2016 the brewery was still bottling beer.

Pahiatua's broad Main Street is three chains wide and was a result of 19th century planning to put the railway line through the middle of the town. Fortunately the railway line went around the town in 1897, leaving Pahiatua blessed with a substantial green area given over to trees and rose gardens.

The towns, predominantly single level Art Deco buildings, include a Spanish

ABOVE: Teeth and Health. The former Dentist Chambers in Main Street was constructed in 1934 by William Hall-Watson who arrived in Pahiatua around 1930. Spanish Mission was reflected in the design of this small facility. The former Plunket Rooms next door provided health care advice and support to mothers with infants and young children.

OPPOSITE PAGE: An illustration of the Pahiatua Regent Theatre circa 1950s.

ABOVE: Pahiatua Post Office (1937). The post office was opened on May 14 1937. The cost was £7100 and the associated postmaster's dwelling £1790.

Mission style Dental Chambers (1934), a stylish Plunket facility (1926), a small-town modern picture theatre (1940), a Stripped Classical post office (1937), a Classical influenced Pahiatua Council Chambers (1929) with decorative panels and a Stripped Classical former National Bank. A large number of the commercial buildings in the main street date from the 1930s to 1940s with many still possessing the original shop windows. The town also possesses numerous industrial garages and workshops from the same period.

Also noteworthy is the Pahiatua Town Bridge (1932) that has a Historic Place Category Listing of 1. This elegant bowstring arch bridge has curved and moulded detailing, entrance wall, Art Deco lamp posts, and bevelled edges. It was the first to be constructed by Fletcher Challenge who in the mid-1930s diversified their activities to include bridge construction. The Pahiatua Town Bridge preceded other bowstring arch bridges built by the company, and was the third bridge of this type constructed in New Zealand.

ABOVE: The fine Art Deco Pahiatua Bridge built in 1932 for the sum of £14,000.

FAR LEFT: The Pahiatua public toilets with its rhomboid window and stepped supports is a unique addition to Pahiatua's collection of built heritage.

LEFT: The Tui brewery with the Mangatainoka River in the foreground.

BOTTOM LEFT: The Pahiatua Council Chambers, 1929 decorated with Classical motifs of cornucopia and roses.

PHOTOGRAPHY: GERRY PARKER

Auckland

A rt Deco and related architecture of New Zealand's largest city includes a number of significant multi-level commercial buildings in the city centre. Since the 1930s Auckland's population has increased exponentially. Accelerated urban growth and the dissolution of political and borough boundaries have changed the identity and physical appearance of what are now regarded as suburbs of a greater Auckland City. The distribution of Art Deco buildings within these former suburbs is sporadic and no Auckland suburb, or former borough, could be characterised as possessing an Art Deco precinct. New suburbs to the west in Henderson and both north and south, and the suburbs of Manukau and Manurewa were still largely rural in the 1930s. Stripped Classical post offices abound and there are the multi-storeyed buildings of Queen Street that are of national significance. However amongst the domestic architecture of Auckland, a large number of Art Deco style houses have been constructed within the suburbs of Point Chevalier, Mission Bay and New Lynn in particular. The Art Deco styles represented range from 1920s Californian bungalows to 1930s and 1940s Art Deco buildings.

In the central business district the international styles were not ignored. At 187-189 Queen Street, the former AEPB building (1929) introduced a Chicago-Gothic style of building to the city and was designed to make a memorable contribution to Auckland. Mr WJ Holdsworth the Board's Chairman rationalised the investment by contrasting the potential for an 'extremely plain affair' with 'paying a little extra, we have something which, from an architectural standpoint, will be a prominent feature in the City.'

LEFT: The Auckland Electric Power Board building (Landmark House) represents one of the few examples of Chicago Gothic style skyscraper architecture. Designed by Alva Bartley and Norman Wade and completed in 1929, the highly decorated exterior uses mullions to emphasise its height.

BELOW: The AEPB decorated with lights to welcome Queen Elizabeth II to New Zealand in December 1953.

OPPOSITE PAGE: The spandrel and façade decoration on the AEPB is eclectic with Classical, Persian, organic and natural themes; urns, torches, spirals, scrolls, seashells, wave shapes, and Persian-inspired stars.

PHOTOGRAPHY: JACK MOYLE

ABOVE: One of New Zealand's premier Art Deco buildings, the Civic Theatre in Auckland's Queen Street.

RIGHT: Classical motifs in bas-relief adorn the building parapets and a frieze of cherubs dances in a panel below.

OPPOSITE PAGE: View of heavily ornate interior of the Civic Theatre.

PHOTOGRAPHY: JACK MOYLE

"In many respects" said one report; 'the block looks even more handsome by night than by day, the lighting scheme (featuring pink and pale green) throwing the ornamentation round the cornices and the tower into far greater prominence.' [1]

The floodlighting was comprehensive with over twenty lights apparent as it sought to advertise both the AEPB and the wonderful energy that was electricity.

The ornamentation on the tower made use of cast concrete Persian-influenced motifs that suitably represented electricity and illumination.

While the AEPB building represented an exotic manifestation of Art Deco, the subsequent building of the company's electrical substations in the next twenty years contributed many of Auckland modest Art Deco style utilitarian buildings. Largely modern were permitted a modest amount of decoration to augment their functional plainness. Today the former Auckland Electric Power Board building is known as Landmark House.

The Auckland Civic Theatre at 267 Queen Street, was constructed in 1929 and is an Art Deco building of international status. The building was designed by Charles Bohringer and William T Leighton and was an example of the atmospheric theatre style in which the domed ceiling was painted dark blue, representing a starlit night sky. The theatre came into being due to the initiative of Thomas O'Brien who owned a number of theatres in the Auckland in the 1920s. With finance from Auckland businessmen and the Bank of New Zealand the Queen Street theatre was constructed by Fletcher Construction and was specifically designed for talking pictures. It included a tearoom in its basement, had a rising 'gondola' orchestra pit as well as the second largest Wurlitzer organ in the Southern Hemisphere. It is known for its exotic,

AUCKLAND LIVE

Indian inspired featuring twisted columns and domed ceilings. Statues of a seated Buddha and Abyssinian panthers, contributed to the fanciful ornately-detailed interior borrowed from Moorish styles of turrets, minarets and spires. The exterior of the building featured a corner tower and the façades were decorated with a bas-relief frieze of cherubic figures. The theatre seats 2,378 people and has remained an Auckland landmark since its construction.

The former T&G Building 39-41 Elliott Street was a Renaissance-style building originally constructed in 1910 before it was purchased by the Temperance and General Mutual Life Assurance Society. The company completely rebuilt the building in accordance to their house style. This involved the addition of the two-storey tower in 1930. At the time, the building was considered the tallest in Auckland.

The MLC building built in the 1950s with its clock tower reflected the house style of the head office in Wellington. Its position at the junction of Queen Street and Wakefield Street gives it a commanding place in the city centre.

The former 1YA building (74 Shortland Street) was constructed as a radio-broadcasting station in 1934 and remains one of the few surviving buildings in New Zealand associated with early broadcasting. It was designed by architects Wade and Bartley who had designed the AEPB building five years earlier. With thick walls and few external windows to ensure the building was soundproofed as possible. The 1YA station was the first licensed radio station In New Zealand. The exterior of the building was Romanesque in style with a stepped brick entrance while the interior features many Art Deco elements. In 1960 it became the first operational television station for the New Zealand Broadcasting Service. The building is still in the services of the arts as a gallery and recording studio.

Newmarket's Olympic Swimming Pool

Kaitaia

CLOCK-WISE FROM TOP LEFT:
Stripped Classical Kaitaia Post Office, 1944; BNZ building, 1948; Modern Professional Chambers; understated Premier Buildings façade 1935; and the stepped façade of the Broadway Buildings.

Perhaps Kaitaia's most striking Art Deco building is the BNZ Building at 50 Commerce Street. The building was opened in 1948. Its asymmetry and modern lines as well as a decorative doorway come from a time that hadn't yet relinquished embellishments.

The majority of buildings in Commerce Street date from between the 1920s and 1940s and the street has not been planted with trees or traffic curbing. The Stripped Classical post office (1944) now Kiwibank is almost a mirror image of the one in Kaikohe (1946). The attractive façades of Broadway Buildings and Premier Building (1935) in Commerce Street contribute to a refreshingly intact and unostentatious town centre.

Although the building is not Art Deco in style the 1940 Centennial Memorial Library and Rest Room is notable and now serves as the Far North Regional Museum. The museum is on the corner of South Road and Matthews Ave.

TOP: Kawakawa Theatre as it appears today.

ABOVE: The fine modern Ford's Building (1941).

Kawakawa

The main street of the small Northland town of Kawakawa is divided by a railway line that runs through the middle of the commercial part of town. This track was originally used by locomotives hauling coal and was reopened in 2008.

The main street features two Art Deco buildings of note. The two-storeyed Ford's Building of 1941 is a well-proportioned modern building. It pleasantly complements the Kawakawa Theatre opposite. Their strong presence in the street is es-

tablished by both buildings' height and styling.

The Kawakawa Theatre, known as the 'King's Theatre' was erected in 1937 following the burning down of its predecessor the year earlier. The new theatre was erected at a cost of £6000 and had a seating capacity of 650. The modern façade has been considerably modified and its symmetry altered by the insertion of two octagonal windows. In its heyday the theatre was a social centre for the town and district.

ABOVE LEFT: The illustration shows the original King's Theatre in 1961. From the movies showing, advertised on the posters, it is apparent that British films were still a real presence. From left to right; a war film *Sea of Sand* (1959) starring Richard Attenborough, a mystery, *House of Secrets* (1936), a United States gangster film, *The Boss* (1956), and a social comedy *The Horse's Mouth* (1958) starring Alec Guinness.

Whangarei

Overlooked by a ring of high bush-covered hills, the city's topography is a constant visual presence. A sense of that presence is best gained from Mt Parihaka and the obelisk that is Whangarei's memorial to those New Zealanders who lost their lives in World War Two, and are buried overseas or have no grave. The summit of Mt Parihaka is one of the most spectacular locations for a monument in the country and looks north and west with almost aerial views over the city below. This nationally significant monument was constructed in 1956 and as it looks backwards so does the design. The project was proposed a year after the conclusion of World War II but the memorial was not unveiled until Anzac day 1957. The obelisk was originally designed as a stone column by Mr FD Finch, an architect engaged in Whangarei, but cost ensured a monument conforming to Art Deco principles in materials if not design. The stainless steel sheathed column in which an illuminated metal cross set on a concrete base has pre-cast concrete panels add simple bas-relief decoration to symbolise the land, sea and air forces and combined services. The decoration includes a three-bladed propeller over a sun with rays pointing upwards and an anchor over a portion of sun with rays pointing downward. The sun as a symbol was very much a design trope of the 1920s and 1930s.

Whangarei possesses some fine examples of Art Deco buildings centred on Bank Street, Rust Ave and Dent Street. The most notable and decorative being the former Central Library in Rust Street. This remains the city's most prominent Art Deco buildings. It was

CLOCK-WISE FROM TOP: A view from Mt. Parihaka of Whangarei harbour and south; the base of the memorial showing the inscription; the decorative carving that represents the airforce; view up the steps; the sheathed top of the monument.

LEFT: Bank Street looking south with the buff coloured Stripped Classical Public Trust building in the centre of the image.

ABOVE: Decoration found on the Public Trust Building around the door and on the front façade.

ABOVE: Detail of decoration that appears around the door.

RIGHT & BELOW RIGHT: One of Whangarei's premier Art Deco buildings the old Library building in Rust Street, built in 1936. Now housing an art gallery.

BELOW: Appropriate book motifs for a library.

PHOTOGRAPHY:TERRY MOYLE

opened on November 12, 1936. It was designed by architect Alfred P Morgan and Horace L Massey and was described at the time as being 'the ultimate in modern design both in the building itself and in the interior fittings'. The building was subsequently awarded the NZ Institute of Architects gold medal in 1938. The original building featured a colour scheme that employed tones of warm buff, reddish brown and grey-green. The exterior was in brick with the doors themselves featuring a carved monogram of the Whangarei Borough Council as well as decoration that symbolised literature, law, commerce and industry. The building's appearance was secondary to its interior design. The 1931 Hawke's Bay earthquake had made seismic strength an essential consideration and the structure was constructed from reinforced concrete with angle steel being used to reinforce trusses and wall heads.

Located at 69 Bank Street the former Public Trust Office was designed by Wellington architect Stanley W Fearn (1887 -1976) who had designed other buildings for the Public Trust. The design is a four-storey commercial building of Stripped Classical design. The design makes use of columns, pilasters and plastered Classical motifs to create a well-composed and attractive building. The ornamentation around the door and public entrance is observed as the building preceded the similarly lavish use of decoration on the Central Library.

Architect Alfred Morgan contributed a number of significant designs to the Whangarei commercial area that are still standing. The beautiful red brick and plaster Ayling Building on the corner of Rathbone and Cameron Streets proclaimed its year of construction in a winged decoration on the parapet and its name in elegant lettering. Several blocks

ABOVE: The Ayling Building, designed by architect Alfred Morgan.

PHOTOGRAPHY: TERRY MOYLE, JACK MOYLE

ABOVE: JW Court's Building, 1940, originally home to a large department store.

ABOVE RIGHT: Victoria Bridge with Hatea River in the background.

BELOW: The attractive Whangarei Falls, found in the north-eastern suburb of Tikipunga.

further on the corner of Cameron and Walton Streets is the substantial and Moderne former JW Courts Building. As a department store it was one of the largest in Whangarei at the time, with showrooms and office space for staff and management comprising 10,000 square feet. This two-storeyed Streamline ferro-concrete building contributed an essential modernity to Whangarei that sits well with the buildings of recent times. The new Whangarei Police Station has been designed in complete sympathy with the 1930s building. Another contribution of Morgan to Whangarei during the 1930s was to design the distinctive ornamentation of Victoria Bridge (1936) that spans the Hatea River. Together with RP Worley the consulting engineer they were the architects for the project. The bridge construction was overseen by the borough engineer, Mr. HW Cormack. The 170 foot reinforced concrete bridge is in three spans and is still in service today; augmented by a canopy-covered pedestrian bridge.

The bridge is visible from Bank street overlooking the Laurie Hall Park as is the former Whangarei Harbour Board Building dating from 1923. An addition sympathetic to the earlier design, with a nautical quality, was built in the 1970's.

Whangarei's Bank Street with its elevated viewpoint and collection of well-designed heritage buildings is the undisputed town centre. From here the green areas leading down to Riverside Drive and the curvaceous 1936 Victoria Bridge are overlooked. The elegant ferro-concrete Victoria bridge shows restrained styling in its pillars. The four Art Deco lights surmounting Classical pillars on a stepped plinth add the expected decorative touch.

ABOVE: A contemporary illustration of the Harbour Board building, viewed from the Victoria Bridge, Whangarei.

Dargaville

The picturesque town of Dargaville on the Northern Wairoa retains the charm of an earlier time in New Zealand. The town has several substantial two-storeyed buildings dating from the early part of the twentieth century. Dargaville's elevated position above the Northern Wairoa River provide ample views of the striking rural, mountain and river landscape surrounding the town. In the main street there are several shop buildings from the 1920s and 1930s, including one with a fine stepped modern façade. The Williams, Ball & Fannon building was built in 1924 and has a decorated façade suiting its original purpose as a tailoring firm. Both tailoring shops in the Waikato town of Huntly feature similarly decorated façades. Jack Fannon, whose name is on the building, retired age 90 from the still operating menswear shop in 2014, after 73 years with the same firm. In the early days the business was dominated by tailoring and latterly by selling menswear which it does to this day.

Wellsford

Located on State Highway One, the rural town of Wellsford is the northern-most town in the Auckland region and has long been associated with travel too and from Whangarei and Northland.

Wellsford makes no pretensions of being an Art Deco destination. Many travellers drive past oblivious to the small office building built in 1936 in the main street. Between two modern buildings its plaster façade provides a simple and well proportioned Art Deco presence. The office front makes full use of Modernist symbolism in bas-relief augmented by the angles on the roof parapet and curved door pediment. The building, now an accountancy firm, quietly contributes to the main street as well as being a reminder of Wellsford's direst of days. During the devastating blaze of December 13, 1955, several of Wellsford's commercial buildings were destroyed. The small Art Deco building marks the point at which the fire was defeated.

PHOTOGRAPHY: TERRY MOYLE

Hamilton

amilton's Art Deco heritage is concentrated in the development of Garden Place during the late 1930s through to the 1950s. In the 1930s the Hamilton Borough Council's concerns were about modernising the city and responding with infrastructure that would accommodate the changes anticipated for the growing city.

Earthquakes led directly to the construction of Napier and Hastings Art Deco precincts simply because of the sudden loss of a town centre and the need for a replacement. If there was no pressing need then change proceeded at its own pace. For Hamilton the

earth was to be moved by human labour and machinery. Before 1940 the flat area known as Garden Place in the Hamilton centre was originally a sizeable hill, with houses and a large pine tree. The removal of the hill in the late 1930s was a major earthworks project that changed the appearance and orientation of Hamilton's central business precinct. It opened up the potential for a business district in the centre of town rather than to the south where the former post office and Bank of New Zealand were originally established.

Around the new area square, created by the removal of the hill, were constructed a

TOP & ABOVE: The Stripped Classical Hamilton Chief Post Office 1940. Art Deco fittings above the entrance.

TOP: Hamilton Chief Post Office Victoria Street, circa 1940s.

ABOVE RIGHT: The CML Insurance building, depicted here in the 1970s.

ABOVE: Taken from the post office this view includes the carpark in the foreground the rose garden and sundial at Garden Place, on the left the CML Building, Armstrong Motors Ltd and the National Insurance Building, circa late 50s early 60s.

OPPOSITE PAGE: Depicted as it was in the 1950s Armstrong Motors Ltd, and the National Insurance Company Ltd building.

number of Art Deco style buildings. These were the new Hamilton Chief Post Office (1940), the Wilber Buildings (1940), the five level Modernist CML Insurance building (1954) and the demolished Streamline Moderne Ford dealership Armstrong Motors (1945) which were constructed on the southern of the new square. The National Insurance building (1954) on the corner of Caro Street and Alexandra Street and the MLC building (1957) on the north-western corner of Garden Place were late additions to Hamilton's central business district. The 1950s insurance buildings were the last additions to modern town centre. The Hauraki Building (C1939), since demolished, was probably the first in Garden Place with a Modern façade. It was built on the northern side next to Pascoes Building and had been operated as a garage prior to the removal of the hill.

The most stately building was the new Stripped Classical Chief Post Office at 346 Victoria Street which had taken two and a half years to construct. The building was sheathed in Hinuera stone sourced locally. Using local materials was consistent with both architectural ideals and the practice of the Government architect. The building featured a spectacular dome comprising individual portions of glass. A Hamilton contractor Bill Young constructed the 93-tonne dome ceiling made up of 1600 circular glass bricks carried out the task. At the time regarded as the second largest dome of its type in the British Empire. The dome remains visible in the considerably modified building of the present day. It was impressive enough, as was the building, for the Postmaster Mr Webb to effusively claim at it's opening that it was the finest in the world.[1]

RIGHT: The former Wilbur Buildings circa early 1950 and OPPOSITE 1967. These buildings are on the south-east corner of Garden Place.

ABOVE: Victoria Bridge, originally known as the Hamilton Traffic Bridge, is a steel arch bridge constructed in 1910.

The former Wilber Buildings were a line of commercial offices and shops occupying the south-east corner of Garden Place. In the 1960s the building acquired another level and the stepped parapet and flagpole was reinterpreted. Replacement of glazing on the second floor and remodelling of the corner of the building has changed the buildings external appearance. Constructed immediately adjacent is the pleasingly shaped Modern former CML building now serving as apartments with the addition of small balconies. Next to the CML building, the demolished Moderne-style Ford building, Armstrong Motors (later Fairview Motors) appear to have installed the Moderne style façade in 1945. The business had been established in the area previously. It was a car salesman's dream location as the cleared area known as garden place was known for many years as 'carpark place', being used for much needed parking in the young and rapidly growing town. The National Insurance Company Ltd building with its Juliet balconies overlooking the car park arrived belatedly in 1954. In 1957 the MLC building was constructed with its decorative Classical sculpture and the motto 'Unity is Strength'.

While the construction of Hamilton's town centre proceeded well into the 1950s, the buildings of the insurance institutions looked to the past and to their identity for their design direction. The National Insurance building of New Zealand constructed in 1954 with its clock tower and persistence with decoration looks more a building of the 1930s than the mid-1950s. Both the CML building and MLC building are retrospective designs influenced by the styles of established institutions. The Art Deco styles contained in Garden Place, certainly in the period during the 1950s, constituted a precinct of Stripped Classical-Moderne style multi-storeyed commercial buildings.

The changes capture the transition of a New Zealand town to an idea of an international one. The institutional contribution with their multi-storeyed buildings suggested in a small scale the larger post-war world that New Zealand was no part of, had arrived in Hamilton, Garden Place.

There are some commercial buildings from the 1920s and 1930s in Victoria Street and in Frankton's Commerce Street in a particular. Refurbishment has significantly changed the appearance and internal layouts of many of these buildings although many of the principle features remain unaltered.

The Hotel Riverina (demolished) was an iconic New Zealand Hotel located on the eastern side of Hamilton overlooking the Waikato River. It both represented and characterised the up-to-date Modern hotel being designed for a corner site. The Riverina had full dining facilities and luxury accommodation. The ferro-concrete hotel was

constructed in 1950 and became a landmark in Hamilton on the corner of Grey Street and Clyde Street. The name RIVERINA was illuminated at night.

Hamilton's Frankton suburb features a number of surviving Art Deco buildings. Commerce Street replicates a small town street with several two-storey buildings from the 1920s to 1930s. The junction of Commerce Street and High Street features the beautiful Spanish Mission styled Hotel Frankton constructed in 1929. With its atmospheric view facing west over the Railway lines and two-storey period buildings opposite, this is one of Hamilton's more evocative corners.

Frankton also possesses an Art Deco garage from 1930s. The building at 150 Columbo Street is a fine example of an early garages from the 1920s and 1930s with brick construction, plastered over and a brick pillar canopy. The parapet of the main

CLOCK-WISE FROM TOP: The Hotel Riverina illustrated as in the early 1970s, The Hotel Riverina in the 1960s, an image of the Art Deco Fairfield Bridge from the 1940s.

building shows some decorative elements not connected with the building's function. The garage was operated for many years by Mr Brian Jesty.

Hamilton's Art Deco built heritage includes the Fairfield bridge (139m) which spans the Waikato River at the northern end of Victoria street crossing to the east to connect with River Road. The three span tied-arch bridge was the fourth largest concrete tied-arch bridge in New Zealand. Construction by Roose Shipping commenced in August 1934 and was completed by 1937. The pierced balustrades are a notable de-

sign feature that add to the aesthetics of this historic structure.

The Fairfield's bridges idyllic park setting and sheer elegance have made it a Waikato icon. Utility is its purpose and the bridge design by Stanley Jones of Jones and Adams, Auckland would provide access to the city for the rapidly expanding northern parts of Hamilton. In 1937 the bridge was part of a three-pronged development scheme being championed by the Hamilton Borough Council; the other two projects being the removal of Garden Place Hill and the lowering of the railway line at Hamilton.

ABOVE: Hotel Frankton in the 1970s.

LEFT: An illustration of the Jestys Art Deco garage in Frankton Junction as it appeared in the 1960s.

Raglan

PHOTOGRAPHY: TERRY MOYLE

The attractive Raglan Municipal Building (1928) at Bow Street was built after a fire destroyed the previous municipal chambers. The fire in March 1927 destroyed both chambers and two shops. The new building was constructed in ferro-concrete and comprised the main Town Hall, boardroom and library, ladies' rest room and dressing rooms. Off the hall was a supper room and kitchen. The style of the building features a prescient Modernist entrance way that looks forward to styles of the late 1930s. Framed by phoenix palms the building contributes an Art Deco element in the small-scale mixture of commercial and service buildings of Raglan's main street.

PHOTOGRAPHY: TREFOR WARD, CLARE STREET, PIERRE

Te Awamutu

The historic town Waikato town of Te Awamutu to the south of Hamilton with its pleasant rose gardens, has heritage buildings dating back to the mid-nineteeth century, notably in Alexandra Street. St. Johns Anglican Church which was completed in 1853, was built for the Church Missionary Society and is the oldest surviving building in the Waikato.

Te Awamutu town centre has a fine collec-tion of single and two-storey Art Deco com-mercial buildings. These include a 1930s post office, a 1930s Streamlined style hotel and 1930s picture theatre. Besides Napier and Hastings, there are few New Zealand towns with largely intact two-storey 1930s streets.

Although many of the town's buildings are undated their style indicates the 1920s and 1930s Te Awamutu underwent a major re-building of its town centre.

CLOCK-WISE FROM TOP: Art Deco glass in Te Awamutu shopfront, 1930s Te Awamutu Post Office; the Regent Theatre; the modern looking Commercial Hotel on Alexandra Street.

OPPOSITE PAGE: Illustration of the demolished Te Awamutu Hotel.

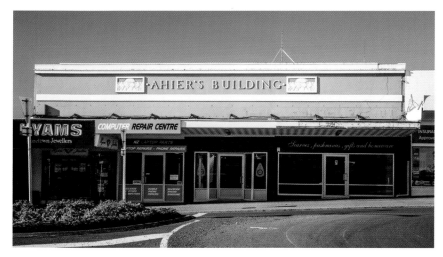

FROM THE TOP: 1930s Stripped Classical Regal Chambers, Market Street; Burchell's Buildings built in 1924 alongside the later Spanish Mission influenced Thompson Bros Building 1937 and Burns House 1936; the attractive Ahier's Building on the corner of Arawa Street.

The former post office (1938) on the junction of Alexandra Street is visible for a distance on the crest of Arawa Street enabling some dominance for the otherwise low profile ferro-concrete building. The post office is Stripped Classical in style. The façade decoration is a rare departure from the usual organic motif and symbols and depicts a pair of old-time telephones bisected by a telephone pole. The use of decoration to show modern progress and machines was more evident in United States buildings than in New Zealand.

The Art Deco part of Te Awamutu might be said to start from the corner of Redoubt Street and Arawa Street and through to Alexandra Street. The buildings that come before the post office date from the 1920s and 1930s. After the post office, the Burchell's Buildings (1924) and Burns House (1936) and Thompson Brothers building (1937) with their matching oriel windows, define the town centre.

Continuing on Alexandra Street the Commercial Hotel (1937) shows the Modern style favoured for corner sites.

Then the still operating and very fine Regent Theatre (1932) with some Stripped Classical elements.

In Market Street, the handsome, Regal Chambers, 34 Market Street and the plainer Market Buildings, their styling both suggesting 1930s designs.

On northern side of Alexandra Street is the plain Heathcote Appliances (Eastern side) Gifford Buildings (1923), the Lims Building (c1930s) with attractive deco façade, the decorated Spinleys Building (c1920s) and the Modern Coronation Building (1953).

The façade of the Te Awamutu Hotel (1935) echoed the oriel windows of Burns House and the Thompson Brothers building. The demolishing of the building diminished the particularly fine 1930s character of the town centre.

Thames

The scenic and historic gold mining town of Thames enjoyed a town centre where many hotels flourished. Art Deco buildings arrived with the introduction of Thames new post office in 1938 and the building of the Hotel Imperial on Pollen Street in 1937. The Modern hotel constructed in concrete was a large building on the corner during a time described as a mild boom in the Thames economy with an acute housing shortage.

The new hotel was understood to have cost a sizeable £10,000 with hot and cold water in each bedroom, and was hailed as being in accordance with the spirit of the times.

On August 4 1937 the old Salutation Hotel was destroyed. The new hotel at 400 Mary Street was to be a Moderne styled, two-storeyed, reinforced concrete building

ABOVE: The Hotel Imperial with a view of the bush-clad hills in the background

with public and private bars. The building was expanded shortly after and the *Thames Star* of January 18, 1954 reported in detail on the décor and the fittings. The exterior of the earlier building is described as a 'pinky shade' while for the new building a medium grey shade had be chosen. The architects of the building were Wade and Bartley. This partnership was also responsible for Auckland's De Bretts Hotel, the 1YA building (1935) and the Auckland Electric Power Board Building in 1930.

LEFT: The Salutation Hotel. Thames at 400 Mary Street.

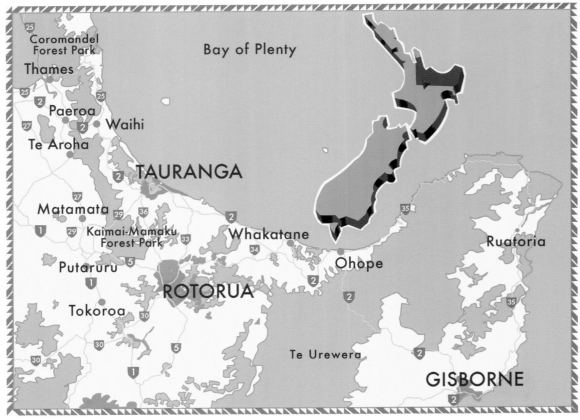

CLOCK-WISE FROM LEFT:
Aurora Theatre; the terrazzo
floor in the theatre; the former
Stripped Classical post office;
former Bank of New Zealand
building.

Paeroa

Paeora streets have a small town Art Deco character and range from buildings constructed during the Victorian era to Art Deco related buildings of the 1920s and 1930s. The town has a cluster of large two-storeyed buildings around the former Paeroa Post Office (1926) at 101 Normanby road. The dominant Aurora Theatre (Regent Theatre) was built in 1927 by Percy Jennings who made his own projectors for use in the cinema. It was leased to Kerridge Odeon in 1938 becoming the Regent, finally closing in 1980. Adjacent is Paeroa's best Art Deco building, the former Bank of New Zealand. Richard Atkinson Abbott (1883-1954) designed the Streamline Modernist building. The bank was constructed by PW Peate and was opened on August 18, 1941. Abbott

was a leading Auckland architect responsible for designing the Spanish Mission Auckland Grammar Buildings, the monument on One Tree Hill as well as BNZ designs including the BNZ building in Warkworth. The Paeroa building is one of the finer Art Deco buildings in the Waikato region. The two-storey building with the Juliet balcony and Stripped Classical entrance is surmounted by simple Māori motif. The grandness and lines of former bank and post office, are in contrast to Paeroa's single-storey buildings, with several Art Deco and Modernist façades.

A retail shop at 66 Belmont Road displays a noticeably zigzag Art Deco façade. The building was designed in 1932 and was originally a bicycle shop.

Te Aroha

ABOVE: The Moderne Te Aroha Borough Council Chambers opened in August 1938. The architect was Mr. HT Barns.

The town of Te Aroha's backdrop is the 952 foot Mount Te Aroha of the Kaimai Range that divides the Waikato from the Bay of Plenty and Tauranga. At the town's feet the Waihou river. Te Aroha's most famous resident is Mokena Hau, the soda geyser. Its Edwardian pavilion, and pleasant gardens set under the tree-covered mountain range, provide elevated views over the broad Waikato Plains and the distant ranges to the west. Te Aroha's Memorial Art Deco town clock set against the huge landscape and early twentieth century buildings is not out of place. Its dominance seems in proportion to the landscape and it is rewarded the most prominent site in the town. The clock tower was started in 1947 and completed in 1955. It is dedicated to the memory of servicemen from the district who fell in the Second World War; a fact made poignant as it situated to be illuminated by facing the setting sun. The hint of a battlement on the tower of Te Aroha's parapet also suggests a design created with a certain knowledge of the historic Firth Tower. This unique Victorian concrete defensive tower was built in 1882. The Firth tower still stands, 34 kilometres to the south near Matamata, as a museum.

The Thames Valley Drainage Board Office in Rewi Street is a notable small Art Deco commercial building with dentil moulding and pillars. It was constructed in 1936.

Waihi

Like Thames, Waihi had established itself largely on its gold mining industry. With labourers came the inevitable hotels. Generously endowed with hotels, the social consequences of drink saw the growth of the Temperance movement. In 1938 The Temperance Union in Waihi expressed their concern at the 'probability of a hotel being erected on the corner of Seddon and Haszard Streets, Waihi' instead of the old site at the corner of Seddon and Devon Streets. The former Commercial Hotel had burned to the ground on June 19, 1938. In any case the opposition proved too much for the owner and he rebuilt the hotel on the original site. The single level building is an attractive Art Deco building dating from 1939 with the Spanish Mission influence most apparent. The porch is accessed through three round arches with the buildings name reproduced in large metal Art Deco lettering.

The phoenix palms that line the road into Waihi from the west do much to affirm the style of the Hotel.

ABOVE: The Commercial Hotel in Waihi is the historic gold-mining town's most obvious Art Deco building.

PHOTOGRAPHY: RODNEY GIDDENS

Katikati

ABOVE: Katikati's War Memorial Hall at night.

Katikati is a small rural town in the Bay of Plenty.

Although not an Art Deco building, the Katikati Memorial Hall's modern appearance and decorative parapet typify the retrospective design of many monuments constructed to commemorate the men from the town and district lost in the First World War. The project was initiated in 1943. The architect was Mr GW Johnston and Mr HDR Rayment's building company carried out the construction. The clearing, earthworks and metalling were carried out by local labour. The building was opened on October 4, 1954 and in 2014 the Memorial Square in front of the building was opened to commemorate the centennial of the commencement of World War One.

LEFT: Early example of Stripped Classical seen in the Mokoia Buildings, 1923.

BELOW LEFT: Central Chambers 1930.

BELOW RIGHT: Modern and simply decorated the 'Rotorua Buildings' from the 20s.

OPPOSITE PAGE: Front elevation of the Rotorua Police Station which was built in 1941.

The Art Deco and Modern Blue Baths (1933) bring to mind the intrigue with glamour that dominated the interwar years. The Blue Baths were built in the typically Classical style of spa pavilions of that era. Designed by Government architect JT Mair during the Depression the baths were regarded as the height of modernity and as an asset for the entire nation.

While being the most conspicuous example of 1930s construction in Rotorua, the town centre also was undergoing expansion and modernising. Many of the original build-ings from the 1920s through to the 1940s have survived. The stylish façades add to the vintage appeal of the tidy town centre. The most notable Art Deco building constructed is the former Rotorua Police Station (1941). With red brick and plastered façades the most conspicuous part of the design was the use of koruru (Māori heads) and patterns in the frieze decoration.

Despite its role as upholding the laws of the nation, the new building was rightly considered beautiful and envy was expressed by Auckland MPs at the time in their quest for

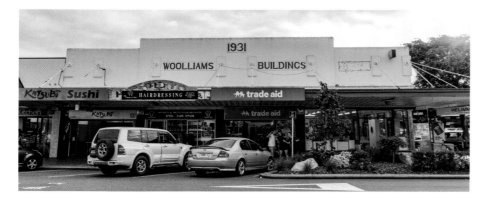

their own modern Auckland Police Station. The building being on the northeast corner of Haupapa and Tutanekai Streets and its appearance was such that people are said to have mistaken the building as a library. Designed by Government architect JT Mair it featured walls 18 inches thick and was made of reinforced concrete with a brick veneer. Māori motif and Art Deco are rare and the building was one of the last for John Mair in the role of Government architect, he would retire from that role in 1941.

Over the door of the former police station is a handsome Royal Coat of Arms carved in stone by an Auckland sculptor Mr RO Gross.

Tutanekai Street
Jubilee Building (1935) at 1202 Tutanekai Street.
Mokoia Buildings (1923) at the corner of Tutanekai and Hinemoa Streets, Central Chambers, 1215 Tutanekai Street, Inverness Building, 1221 Tutanekai Street, Woolliams Buildings (1931) at 1174 Eruera Street.

Arawa Street
Kusabs Building, 1154 Arawa Street.
The Fat Dog, 1611 Arawa Street.
Dannefærd Building (1934), 1157 Arawa Street.
Hannah's building (1937), 1151 Arawa Street.
Rotorua's central business district has most of the city's earlier commercial buildings. These include the former Hannah's Building (1937), at 1151 Arawa Street. Hannah's footwear company is an established brand in New Zealand's retail

PHOTOGRAPHY: PETRA ZOE

TOP LEFT: The Jubilee Building featured a modern stepped façade and lettering.

CENTRE LEFT: The former bank of at 1251 Tutanekai Street was built in 1937 with an attractive Art Deco door lintel.

LEFT: Woolliams Building, 1931.

postal wharenui (1940) and Rotorua's Police Station (1940) the Māori design elements are minimal but strategically placed. Here they recall the carved verticals of a meeting house. The East Coast Commission building (1936) was designed by LG West, Son and Hornibrook of Gisborne and Palmerston North. The East Cost Commission was involved in assisting the management and development of substantial Māori land holdings on the East Coast. Despite its small scale it is a rare example of what could be called Māori Deco applied to a Modern style building.

The demolished Bathing Pavilion was designed by local architect and built in the 1950s. This featured an upper story with glazed semi-circular rooms and an exposed upper deck with an elevated view south towards Young Nick's Head. The pavilion was part of life at the beach of Waikenae, where people stayed at the camping ground and it served the people of Gisborne and added much nautical style to the beach front. The handsome Street. Andrews Presbyterian Church in Childers Road still stands. It was designed by Frederick Forge who carried out a lot of design work in the Bay of Plenty, East Coast and Hawke's Bay area.

Peel Street has a number of attractive Art Deco buildings. These include the M. Zemba Limited Building (1937) at 63 Peel Street and the large Security Building at 58–60 with its outstanding windows and Modernist styling.

OPPOSITE PAGE: The demolished Gisborne Bathing Pavilion, illustrated in the 1950s.

Ruatoria

Ruatoria Garage in the 1940s. Even the most remote township in New Zealand was connected to the modern theme. The stylish façade of the garage of this former petrol station gave the right impression of progress even though the design was created with maximum economy. The garage was still pumping gas into the twenty-first century.

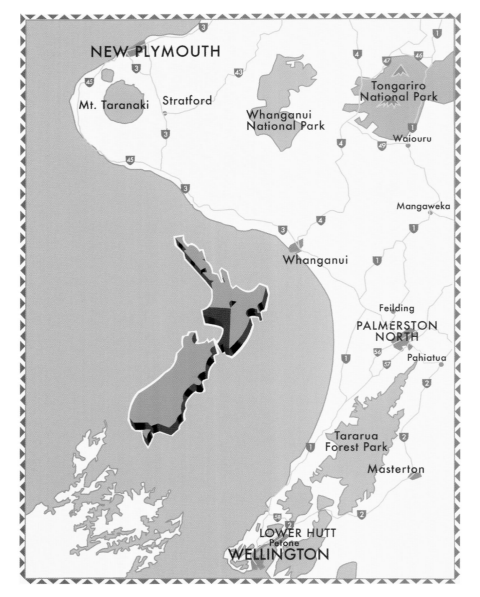

NEW PLYMOUTH

Mt. Taranaki Stratford

Whanganui National Park

Tongariro National Park

Waiouru

Mangaweka

Whanganui

Feilding

PALMERSTON NORTH

Pahiatua

Tararua Forest Park

Masterton

LOWER HUTT
Petone
WELLINGTON

New Plymouth

New Plymouth, with its dramatic, inescapable backdrop of Mount Egmont (Mt Taranaki) and its location on New Zealand's west coast, has much to offer in built heritage. Along with the contemporary mirrored Len Lye Centre (2015) named for one of New Plymouth's most celebrated artistic talents, and the elaborate Victorian White Hart Hotel (1886), it also possesses many buildings constructed in the 1920s and 1930s. A walk down Devon Street provides the experience of a very intact mid-twentieth century town precinct with no less than three heritage theatres. Many of New Plymouth's buildings have dec-

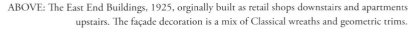

ABOVE: The East End Buildings, 1925, orginally built as retail shops downstairs and apartments upstairs. The façade decoration is a mix of Classical wreaths and geometric trims.

RIGHT: Decorative moldings on the King's Building, 1927.

OPPOSITE PAGE: A contemporary illustration of Brougham Street, with the former National Bank of New Zealand, designed by architects Mitchell and Mitchell of Wellington now the ASB, and King's Building on the right. Len Lye's 'Wind Wand' can be seen in the background.

ABOVE: The St. Aubyns Chambers building occupies the corner of St. Aubyn Street and Queen Street and is opposite the Cenotaph. It was orgininally built in 1927 as flats and a service station. The architects were Messenger, Griffiths and Taylor.

RIGHT: Although hard to see now through the trees the former Mayfair Theatre utilised coloured cement to brighten its façade.

orated façades. These range from simple geometric forms to more elaborate borrowings from Mayan designs. The use of decorative elements is conspicuous enough to be called a characteristic of New Plymouth Art Deco buildings.

The YWCA & YWCA Community House (1929) is one of New Plymouth's most distinctive Art Deco buildings. The façade was designed by Taranaki architect, Thomas H Bates. Another Thomas Bates building, Masters Ltd (1930) in Egmont Street, is a strong design with simple decorative elements, as is Kurta's Building (66-68 Devon Street).

The Economic (128 Devon Street) is a former drapers shop constructed in 1936.

The Building Investment Ltd (1941) at 113 -115 Devon Street features a façade with Moderne style decoration. Its history included a period as a garage and in the 1930s part of the building housed a miniature golf course.

The National Bank building (1939) at 66 Devon Street, on the corner of Brougham Street, is designed in the Stripped Classical style adopted by the bank during this period. A decorative frieze on the parapet ensures the building is sympathetic to the King's building (1927) opposite. The architects were Mitchell and Mitchell, Wellington.

The State Theatre dates from 1934 with the first screening on March 1935. The building features a decorated pattern on the parapet and was highly sympathetic with other buildings in the street. It was designed by George E Tole.

Mayfair Theatre (1937) at 67 Devon Street West was originally built in 1916 and in 1937, Thomas Bates redesigned the façade and entrance. The use of coloured cement gives this handsome building a predominantly rose hue. The Art Deco elements include geometric motifs on the window heads and parapet.

ABOVE: The YWCA & YWCA Community House in Powderham Street has a Stripped Classical façade and decoration that is Mayan-influenced.

RIGHT: Sole Bros building on the corner of Devon Street West and Currie Street. Originally built as shops and offices. The architect was FE Gooder of Wellington.

BELOW: The simply modern State Theatre 1935.

BOTTOM: The former LH Johnson garage was built in the late 1920s. The architects were Messenger, Griffths and Taylor.

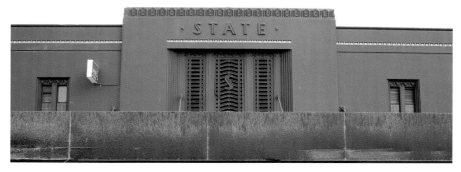

The C.C. Ward building (1933) at Devon Street has largely been unaltered since it was built. It features simple decorative elements.

The former Taranaki Daily News (1937) on the corner of Powderham and Currie Street is one of New Plymouth's more striking buildings designed in an eclectic mix including Mayan decoration. This and decorative ironwork contribute to its impression of importance as the media centre of its time.

The National Insurance Building at 36 Brougham Street was built in 1938 and shows Modern and Art Deco influences.

The former LH Johnson Motors Ltd (1929) on the corner of Devon Street - Gover Street. is an example of an early garage that included petrol bowser service. The building façade retains simple, modern decoration.

Although architects designing for New Plymouth commercial buildings created little work in Moderne styling (and Spanish Mission is largely absent), the influence of Art Deco is strongly represented and contributes much to the distinctive character of the city centre.

ABOVE: The Taranaki Daily News, built in 1937.

LEFT: The Public Trust Office in Stratford was built in 1924. A Stripped Classical building with Mayan influenced decoration on the tops of the palaters and zig zag pattern above the carved lettering. A large parapet originally topped the façade, which was probably removed for safety reasons after the Hawke's Bay earthquake in 1931. The façade was substantially modernized at the same time.

Whanganui

Whanganui, at the mouth of the Whanganui River on the North Island, is considered one of New Zealand's most beautiful towns. The very intact and, externally at least, original streets of historic 19th and early 20th century buildings contribute to unique town centre. The mix of Victorian and Edwardian freestyle buildings vividly recall an older urban New Zealand. It was both Whanganui's well-established centre and the modest economies of the 1930s that ensured only a few touches of modernity in the established streetscape until late in the decade.

Whanganui's former Chief Post Office at 60 Ridgeway Street was the exception and it was a remarkable building. Drawn up by local architect, Robert G Talboys of RG Talboys and Associates, the Whanganui Chief Post Office was indisputably the most important Whanganui building in the town centre at the time. Construction started in February 1939. The contractor for the £90,000 job was WM Angus of Napier. The new three-storeyed ferro-concrete building was opened on December 11, 1940. Talboy's design was the most ambitious interpretation of Māori culture into a public building at the time. The Stripped Classical building features four columns at the entrance each surmounted by a carved stone koruru head. The *Wanganui Chronicle* (Dec 11 1940) observed that 'The architect is to be complimented on breaking away from the orthodox Greek and Roman Capitals to perpetuate that of his own coun-

ABOVE LEFT: An elevated view of the post office, circa late 50s.

ABOVE: One of the Māori head carvings that form the capitals of the post office Stripped Classical pilasters.

OPPOSITE PAGE: An illustration of the impressive main entrance of the Whanganui Post Office circa 1950s.

ABOVE: A contemporary illustration of the Saint Hill Street entrance called the Golden Gates.

try.' It was a slightly colonial sentiment at a nationalistic time. The country was at war with Germany and the post office was a still not completed. It is a rare example, the most overt perhaps, of Māori motif used as decoration in a public building. The scrolled carvings of a canoe prow are reproduced on the parapet. They represented the analogous role of the canoe and the role in communications played by the modern post office. It was a theme perhaps sought in the four pillars with their respective disembodied heads and protruding tongues. The post office was finished with an attractive pink Hanmer stone base. A more spacious location than Ridgeway street would have better served the imposing appearance of the building. However its role was functional and this was reflected in various modern features. Electricity was used in ways that were considered particularly innovative. Telegrams were delivered to an upper floor by electrically driven tubes, and more than 50 electric clocks were around the building with the aim of ensuring everyone worked to the same time. The heating system involved an electrically-driven pump which claimed to be highly efficient and the basement area was ventilated by electrically powered fans, also considered a notable example of modern technology.

The floor plan shows the multiple function of the post office of the era. There is an abundance of desks set up for the paperwork to be filled out. There are lines of tellers on either side of the building; telegrams, motor registration, mail and postage, freight and mail handling and banking of course.

The Golden Gates at 99 Saint Hill Street were another incursion of modern design in the heart of Whanganui. Work on the gates which lead to Cook Gardens was carried out by relief gangs and was supervised by the Whanganui City Council. The gates were constructed as an upgrade to the Saint Hill entrance that would lead to the South African War obelisk. The project required extensive earthwork preparation to achieve the required gradient of the steps. The Golden Gates (the actual gates were prosaic steel) features a central concave wall with a plaque, flanked by a pair of small and large pilasters on either side. The new gates and their modern-styled stepped walls also served a timely ceremonial purpose. The Golden Gates were

modern because New Zealand's self reflection of the time was as a modern nation. The gates were officially opened in 1940 to mark the Centennial.

Other Art Deco buildings of interest in Whanganui are small-scale. At 37 Quay Street a two-storey concrete building constructed in 1935 features interesting concrete plaster decoration.

59 Victoria Ave is Dustin's building (1895), refurbished in 1939 with a Streamlined Moderne façade with a central pilaster designed by architect Clifton Newton Hood.

Whanganui's Art Deco is what might be called 'Centennial Deco', which saw building construction specifically aimed at New Zealand achieving 100 years as well as having a social directive. Although interwar year buildings are not prevalent, the former Whanganui Chief Post Office should be regarded as one of New Zealand's significant Art Deco buildings.

Mangaweka

The former Langholm Hotel is in the settlement of Mangaweka, in the Manawatu-Whanganui region. Located at 6 Broadway it is a single-storey hotel constructed in a Modern Art Deco style.

It was built in 1946. No longer a hotel it now serves as the Mangaweka Family Lodge with three bedroom family accommodation. Originally established in 1886 the former hotel is directly opposite a two-storey Bank of New Zealand designed in Georgian style. The small street of Broadway has a collection of early 20th century single-story commercial buildings. The authentic Western looking street has been used as a film location in the past.

PHOTOGRAPHY: SIMON BURT

Palmerston North

Palmerston North's Regent Theatre is the city's most compelling Art Deco building. Not only is it an exquisite theatre, inside and out, it is the spirit of Palmerston North. After the building closed it was purchased by the Palmerston North City Council. A massive fundraising undertaking from the community, with money from both the New Zealand Lotteries Grants Board and the local Council, saw meticulous restoration and refurbishment work carried out. The original architect, Charles Hollingshead, had described the interior of the theatre as based on a fifteenth century Florentine manor house. It is a must-see destination for anyone interested in Art Deco with a taste for the exotic that permeated the 1920s and 1930s.

The ziggurat styled Art Deco tower of the T&G (Temperance and General Mutual Life Assurance Society) was constructed in 1938. Palmerston North's building at 14-18 Broadway Avenue maintains its dominance in the

THE SQUARE, PALMERSTON NORTH, New Zealand

P.P.L. HASTINGS. P.677

still relatively low profile skyline. The Auckland and Wellington T&G buildings have since been shrunken by the taller architecture that surrounds them. Using the Melbourne firm of A&K Henderson, a "house" style was developed for the company that included the distinctive, ziggurat tower. Palmerston North's T&G building was built toward the end of this period. The project was supervised by the architectural firm of Mitchell and Mitchell. T&G building was the tallest at the time of construction and featured fully automatic lifts in the tower. The building is now known as Ansett House.

Ward Brothers Building 213 Cuba Street was constructed in 1935 for the Palmerston North brothers William Ercott Ward and Edward E Ward. The small but conspicuous building features an Art Deco oriel window, stepped parapet and zigzag and chevron motifs. Considered one of Palmerston North's best Art Deco buildings the building was designed by the architectural firm of LG West, Son & Hornibrook.

The former CM Ross and Co Building 1928 was designed in the Chicago style. The department store's tearooms were considered the best in the city. Today it has been refurbished

ABOVE: An early 70s postcard of Palmerston North looking north down Broadway Avenue, the dominant T&G Building (now called Ansett House) is at 14-18 Broadway Avenue.

OPPOSITE PAGE: The imposing tower of the T&G building.

PHOTOGRAPHY: HEATHER GLASGOW

into the Palmerston North Library. The deconstructed redesign of the building in 1996 was created by architect Ian Athfield.

Former Palmerston North Police Station was completed in 1939. This reinforced concrete Stripped Classical style building was designed by the Office of the Government architect under the direction of John Mair. The decorative elements are far more pared back than for the Rotorua Police Station. Here restricted to an extended Māori kōwhaiwhai parapet and a prominent hand-modelled coat of arms. Although the use of Māori Deco was extremely rare in public buildings the design is timely, a result of the bi-cultural consciousness aroused by New Zealand's pending centennial. A porch was added to the police station entrance in the 1990s but the exterior remains largely unmodified.

Palmerston North's Regent Theatre (1930) was designed by Melbourne architect Charles Hollingshead. Together with AH Walkely the pair were the principal architects for JC Williamson's chain of Australasian theatres. The interior of the theatre was lavish and included the vaulted marble staircase, the kōwhaiwhai design on the mezzanine ceiling. The auditorium featured a large fresco by the Australian scenic artist W Colman. The exterior in contract presented a restrained modern theatre with a stepped parapet and shallow relief chevron decoration.

The Palmerston North Council Chambers were designed in 1945 by Palmerston North architect Reginald Thorrold Jaggard. However part of the building was erected in 1923 and was incorporated into the new 1945 building. This design combined Stripped Classical elements with Moderne appearance. The building in the Palmerston North

ABOVE: The Palmerston North Police Station.

OPPOSITE PAGE: The Council Chambers circa 1950s. To the right is the All Saint's Church which is one of Palmerston North's landmark churches, it was completed in 1914 and consecrated in 1916. The large English Gothic style brick building was designed by architect Frederick de Jersey Clere who was responsible for numerous churches in New Zealand. The builder was John Henry Meyer.

CLOCK-WISE FROM ABOVE LEFT: The ladies rest rooms built in the Modern style in 1936. The rooms were later enlarged in 1949, and subsequently in 2004 when an information centre was added; the CM Ross and Co Building, 1928 now the Palmerston North Library; The Ward Bros building in Cuba Street was built in 1935.

town centre brought a very different style of building to the streetscape around the square. The contractor for the new civic chambers was McMillan Brothers and the building cost £42,200.

Palmerston North possesses some pleasing accessible Art Deco with the buildings on the north-eastern side of the Square. The 1935 Civic Building and adjacent buildings, provide a view to the Waldegrave Building (1932) in Broadway. Heading north up Broadway one encounters the T&G Building and Regent Theatre at 53 Broadway Avenue.

PHOTOGRAPHY: HEATHER GLASGOW; SIMON BURT

PHOTOGRAPHY: ADAM SIMPSON

Masterton

The Wairarapa Times Age building on the corner of Chapel and Cole Streets is Masterton's best-known Art Deco building. The 1938 building for the newspaper company was designed by the firm Mitchell and Mitchell. The Wellington firm was also responsible for designing Wellington's Central Fire Station, the decoration of which is similar to that on the Masterton building. The modern design arouses maritime associations.

Constructed in reinforced concrete the overall styling suggests Streamline Moderne while the building's chamfered corner, Juliet balcony, pillars and flagpole are conservative elements. The building was extended in 1961 to provide offices for editorial staff, a photographers' room, and two darkrooms.

The former CML building at 4 Perry Street is almost identical in style to the CML building in Nelson and was constructed cir-

ABOVE: The former CML building, Perry Street.

LEFT: At 285 Jackson Street, the current Westpac building, originally constructed as shops in 1939.

OPPOSITE PAGE: Illustration of Petone McKenzies store from 1937. McKenzie's stores were present in many New Zealand towns and cities and were a byword for inexpensive consumer goods.

Notable among the 1930s buildings is 230 Jackson Street, where the former Petone McKenzies Department store was located. John Robert Hugh McKenzie founded the company in 1910, with his first store in Dunedin. McKenzies grew to become a chain of 75 stores in towns throughout New Zealand and remained a household name until the company was taken over in 1980. New Zealanders of an earlier era will recall shopping at McKenzies, which offered a range of low cost, generally small household goods. In the months before Christmas the shops became very busy places and the name 'McKenzies' also became a byword for a budget-conscious type of purchase.

The Petone building features a modern façade designed by architects Haines and Lamb in 1936. The stepped parapet of strong verticals communicated a presence quite different from the Edwardian Free Classical style that had existed previously. The McKenzies branding was particularly evident. The windows were emblazoned with McKenzie's house style and logos. The product range and window displays were similar. Although the former JR McKenzies Petone shared the same style of frontage, the head office building in downtown Wellington building had three entrances. In

Petone there were two and a rare opportunity to design the shop front as a whole. In this instance pairing a stepped entrance with a stepped parapet. Complete with the name JR McKenzies and generous use of company red it made for a distinctive modern retail building with eye-catching window displays.

The UFSD (United Friendly Societies Dispensary Board) building at 249-251 Jackson Street is an attractive Art Deco building. The façade was built in 1936 and was designed by Francis H Swan.

At 278-280 former Willis Dental Surgery is a notable building designed by significant Art Deco architect, Edmund Anscombe. This attractive Art Deco building is designed with Spanish Mission references. The building was constructed in 1934 and built by J H Meyer and Co. Norman Willis remained in the building until the late 1950s however it continued to operate as a dentist until the mid-1970s.

The Moderne style single-level building on the corner at 285 Jackson Street was built in 1939 and was used for shops until the Bank of New South Wales occupied the building. The architect was Francis H Swan and the building contractor was WG Templeton. It featured a stepped central pilaster above the entrance.

tone. The monument features chamfered corners near the top of an octagonal profile. Five semi-circular copper louvers are installed in the corners. The dentilled roof is surmounted by a lamp of remembrance. The Carillon has 65 bells and the original specification was 69.

Smaller scale memorials were built elsewhere in New Zealand, often Classical in execution but often introducing an Art Deco aesthetic inseparable from the gravitas of the structure, memorial garden or obelisk.

Admiring the aesthetics of the tower does not diminish the tremendous significance the memorial had to Wellington and a nation that had lost so many men in the world war of 1914–1918. After restoration work the complex was re-dedicated by Queen Elizabeth II on February 26, 1986. Plans were proposed for a national Tomb of the Unknown Warrier and the tomb was designed by Kingsley Baird. On November 11, 2004 the remains of an unidentified New Zealander who died during the First World War were interred in the tomb.

The Vic (1935), 154-156 Cuba Street, formerly a hotel was designed by James Bennie. It possesses a distinctive façade of stepped decorative forms and zigzag decorations, likewise the James Smith building (1932) on the corner of Cuba and Manners Street. Built in 1907, it was modernised in 1932 to Art Deco appearance. The new façade was designed by King and Dawson. The attractive Wellington Free Ambulance Building (1932) at Cable Street was designed by William Turnbull and features carefully stepped detail and fluted spandrels.

The Stripped Classical former Wellington City Library had an appearance not dissimilar from the style of post offices designed by Government architect, JT Mair.

ABOVE: Hotel Saint George 1930 designed by William Prouse.

THIS PAGE AND OPPOSITE: The terracotta sheathed MLC building.

In this instance the design was created by a partnership of Gummer and Ford and New Plymouth architects, Taylor and Wolfe. The building exterior was designed by Taylor and Wolfe after a competition to determine the winning design. In the 1990s the former library was converted to the Wellington City Art Gallery.

The Hotel Saint George (1930) at 124 Willis Street was designed by William Prouse. An Art Deco hotel in a visual sense, the building's façades and decorative mouldings work as much as the basic forms of the building to suggest a later style. The vigorous stepped linear detail framing the layered pilasters is repeated in the balustrades pierced with a stepped design. The proportion and distribution of the windows, singly, in pairs and trios augmented by raised squares and rectangles add to the visual complexity of this dynamic looking building. The Hotel Saint

143

THIS PAGE: Former Brandon House at 150-152 Featherston Street. This building was designed by architect Francis Stewart and was completed in 1931 for the law firm established by Alfred de Bath Barndon. Notable are the mouldings at the top of both façades and the spandrel panels. The interior includes the rarity of original panelled lifts, machinery and floor indicators.

George was considered Wellington's best hotel and remains a landmark Art Deco building of both the capital and the country.

The South Lambton Quay historic area represents the best group of multi-storey Art Deco buildings in New Zealand. A number of the buildings in the historic area pre-date the 1930s but the South Lambton Quay buildings provide a necessary urban perspective on the New Zealand Art Deco styles, particularly when most town centre's were comprised of single or two-storeyed buildings.

The former Brandon House (1929) at 150-152 Featherston Street was designed by Francis Stewart.

The MLC Building at 231 Lambton Quay was completed for the Australian-based company, Mutual Life and Citizens Assurance Company in 1940. The architects were Mitchell and Mitchell of Wellington. The firm William Angus Ltd of Napier undertook the contract for over £101,494 pounds. The nine-storeyed building was to be faced in terracotta. At the MLC annual general meeting held in Sydney it was reported that the Wellington building was nearing completion and forms an 'outstanding addition to the architecture of the Dominion Capital complete with decorative panels'.[1] The face of the building tower remained empty however and was not filled by the intended clock until 1953. In 1985 the New Zealand branch of the company's operations were purchased by New Zealand Insurance. This severed the company's long association with the building. Similarly styled MLC buildings were constructed in Auckland's Queen Street and Hamilton's Garden Place in the 1950s.

The Prudential Insurance building (1934-35) is one of New Zealand's most spectacular commercial Art Deco buildings located at 332-340 Lambton Quay. The building was designed by the Melbourne firm of Hennessy and Hennessy in association with Wellington architects Gray, Young,

Morton and Young. The building was originally constructed in reinforced concrete that had been coloured to resemble sandstone. Notable is the use of artificial stone facing on the ground floor. This material was known as Benedict stone. The style of the building combines Classical, decorative and Chicago elements in an imposing office building. From a social history point of view, the building's construction was enabled by the government's provision of relief workers. The building as originally built featured four very similar front elevations; the proportion of which has been lost with an additional top storey and other alterations, including the painting over of the coloured cement render, that had been lined to give the appearance of blocks of stone.

South British Insurance Building (1936), 326 Lambton Quay, constructed in coloured ferro-concrete. The Neo-Georgian building features figurative decoration over the windows on the first storey and was designed by Auckland architect MK Daffin. By the mid-1930s the style of the buildings such as this one looked old-fashioned and conservative.

The former State Insurance Building (1940), 143-149 Lambton Quay, is described by Shaw as 'extraordinary', was a remarkable design resolution of a difficult site.[2] The building is outstanding for its physical presence as much as its innovation. The design by William Henry Gummer (1884-1966) and Charles Reginald Ford (1880-1972) resulted in one of New Zealand's best modern buildings. Gummer and Ford designs had included major Auckland projects like the Dilworth Building (1926) and the Classical Wintergarden buildings. They were awarded Gold Medals from the New Zealand Institute of Architects for their designs of the Auckland Railway Station and the Remuera Library. The State Insurance Building is designed as a façade, a 'wavy' face to fit around the corner. The extensive use of glazing and innovative

ABOVE: Flying Boats were the first aitcraft to bring international travel to New Zealand.

The magnifcent Prudential Insurance Building (1934-35) located at 332-340 Lambton Quay. The ornamentation on the spandrels is Mayan infuenced, featuring flowers and fronds.

CLOCK-WISE FROM LEFT: Wellington's multi-storey Art Deco with the MLC building on the far left, next the Prudential building, then the former CBA building, and lastly the South British Insurance building; carved spandrels on the South British Insurance building; the Prudential building just after it was built, the CBA building next door is not in existence.

features such as fluorescent lighting, and fast lifts made the State Insurance building utterly modern. The Government commissioned the building coincidentally with the Centennial year.

The Departmental Building (1940) is New Zealand's most magnificent Modern-style building and a genuine monument that was in keeping with New Zealand's expression of nationhood on display in the Moderne-style pavilion near Rongatai - one of New Zealand's great Art Deco buildings. The building was designed by Government architect John Mair and built by Fletcher Construction between 1939-1941. On the drawing board in 1936 the building was designed to accommodate civil service staff who were currently operating out of rented offices. The huge building looked to the Modernist-styled buildings and hotels of British architects like Francis Lorne. It was the largest office in Wellington at the time and had five acres of floor space. It became the New Zealand Defence Headquarters when World War II arrived. The building became well known outside Wellington with the use of its image in a pioneering New Zealand comedy, '*Gliding On*', which ran for five seasons in the 1970s; the fine aesthetics of the building being presented for a generation as synonymous with bureaucracy and the civil service. In the 1989 the interior of the structure was completely refurbished. If the building had acquired a reputation for bureaucracy it certainly had a deserved one for procedure. At various stages it provided offices for the Birth, Deaths and Marriages Registry of the Justice Department, the Audit Office, the Treasury and as the long-term Headquarters for the New Zealand defence forces.

Nelson

ABOVE: The Nelson State Theatre and Chambers dates from the 1930s. The Theatre was opened in 1936.

Nelson enjoys long hours of sunshine and a strong collection of heritage buildings, including many examples of Art Deco styles.

The prominent corner of Trafalgar and Halifax Streets represented a superb high profile location for the State Chambers and film theatre. The ferro-concrete building was designed by architect H Francis Willis and opened in 1936. The Art Deco Streamline Moderne style of the building transformed downtown Nelson. The building projected a most progressive appearance. Although the building has undergone refurbishments in 1992 the original exterior has been maintained.

H Francis Willis had designed theatres in Christchurch and performed a lot of design work for Amalgamated Theatres (owned by the Noodabe brothers). Willis had designed the well-known series of Spanish Mission style buildings in Christchurch called New Regent Street.

At 86-110 Trafalgar Street is the former States Advances building (1938) designed in a Stripped Classical style. The cement was coloured to imitate sandstone with the base of the building defined by a deeper tone. The building was designed by Government architect JT Mair and is considered a particularly

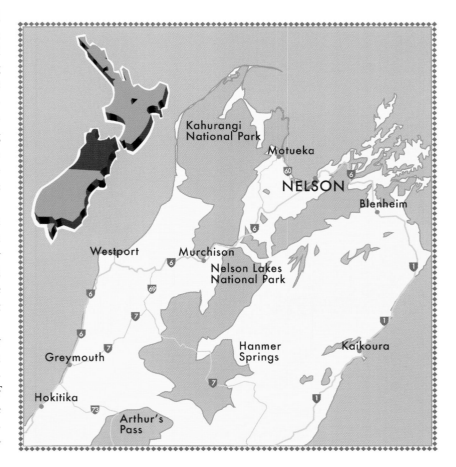

PHOTOGRAPHY: STEPHEN RAINBOW, DR ANN McEWAN

ABOVE: The former State Advances building (Nelson City Council) 106-110 Trafalgar Street showing the liberal use of coloured concrete.

fine design. The building was designed at the same time as the much larger Wellington Government Life headquarters building and has many similarities in overall style, façade treatment and Art Deco decoration.

It features parapet detail of triangles and curves that was common on banks and post offices in the 1930s. The interior features a handsome stairwell designed in Moderne style. The appearance of both the State Advances building and the State Chambers contributed immediately to a new Moderne appearance for Nelson. The former Norwich Union Chambers (1936) and former Public Trust Office (1937) at 173 Hardy Street and 221 Hardy Street respectively consolidated the Art Deco styles in the town centre.

The former Public Trust Office (1937) is a handsome Art Deco building constructed in coloured ferro-concrete. Stripped Classical in style, the building features two dominant plaster floral decorations and stone fac-

ing. A doorway lintel pierced by a geometric pattern adds an impression of richness to a conventional bank building design.

Nelson's appears to be particularly well represented in domestic Art Deco houses. What is also apparent is the Modernist façades of service buildings on Halifax Street. These lesser examples of Art Deco built heritage collectively contribute to the undeniable style and authenticity of Nelson's town centre.

Nelson's former airport building was completed in 1940 for the purposes of commercial air travel. It was an attractive modern Streamline passenger terminal built for the Nelson Harbour Board. It was constructed by B & GT Holbrook Ltd for a contract price of £4345 and work was underway by mid-1939. Designed in accordance with the styling of international airports, Nelson airport and its new Art Deco terminal were promptly requisitioned at the outset of World War II by the Royal New Zealand Air force.

NEW ZEALAND
NELSON

LEFT: The Nelson Cathedral, was started in 1925 and completed in 1965. The Modernist Gothic cathedral's position at one end of Trafalgar Street, and its relationship with the modern appearance of the State buildings, is a defining aspect of the town centre.

BELOW: former Public Trust Office (1937).

Nelson
New Zealand

N.A.C.

BY AIR
Classique

NELSON AIRFIELD

NEW ZEALAND NATIONAL AIRWAYS CORPORATION

NAC
60th Anniversary

De Havilland D.H. 114 Heron 1, Nelson Airport 1955

Lockheed Lodestar,
refueling at Nelson

CLOCKWISE FROM TOP: Nelson's early airport terminal was built in 1939 and was a modern-style air terminal although clearly a small building. The illustration shows the Nelson Airfield in 1955. The aircraft depicted a De Havilland DH 114 Heron operated by New Zealand National Airways Corporation; two small commercial buildings in Vanguard Street. The abundance of Art Deco style domestic buildings also contribute to the Art Deco quality of Nelson.

Passenger services at the building did not commence until 1949, when NAC (National Airways Corporation) occupied the ground floor. The airport terminal building was demolished in 1975 and a new terminal was opened by the Prime Minister Rt Hon Bill Rowling on June 28, 1975.

Nelson's former Colonial Mutual Life Assurance building was completed in 1955. It was designed by the Wellington-based Structon Group. The design was reflective of the International style and strongly resembles the CML building in Masterton. Architecturally it was conservative as most of the Insurance company designs generally were in the 1950s.

The two-storey modern style Post Office Hotel at 122 High Street, Motueka and with the former post office (1943) opposite are notable. The Hotel Motueka (1940) remains the town's most stylish Art Deco building.

TOP: Norwich Union Chambers built in 1936 at 173 Hardy Street.

ABOVE: The former Nelson Fire Station built in 1940 at 5 Halifax Street.

PHOTOGRAPHY: CHARLES RICHARD BRUNING

Westport

One of New Zealand's finest Art Deco buildings, the former Municipal Chambers is a dominant feature of the town of Westport. The building was first proposed in 1936 by the Mayor, Kilkenny. The architect was Mr Archibald MacDonald of whom little is known apart from that he was a resident in Westport for a period. The design was accepted by the council, and ratepayers' support gained, tenders were called for the building in July 1938 and construction began by the end of that year.

In December the former town hall was demolished, and the site was cleared to enable the foundations of the new building to be laid. The chambers were built of concrete and 50 tons of reinforcing steel, it featured rimu in the interior and terrazzo floors. The building was finished in a mustard yellow plaster using Motueka sand, this being a cheap and popular way to simulate the look of sandstone. The building has a Historic Place Category 1 status.

Progress on the building was hindered in part by the rising cost of materials due to the outbreak of the Second World War. In December 1940, the Town Clerk suggested that the back of the building be left unplastered until the entirety was complete as a cost saving measure.

The bulk of the work, apart from the upper part of the clock tower had been completed by April 1940, although finishing touches such as the terrazzo floors and the plastering of all of the exterior were not completed until 1941.

The Moderne style former Buller Municipal Chambers (1940), 161 Palmerston Street is an attractive Art Deco building in which both streamline elements and stepped elements are combined.

The engineer for the project was CF Schadick and the building contractor JS Jackson.

ABOVE: The Buller County Chambers were built in 1940.

OPPOSITE PAGE TOP: Westport Municipal Chambers is one of New Zealand's finest Art Deco buildings.

OPPOSITE PAGE BOTTOM: The Chambers in the 1950s, prior to the planting of the pair of phoenix palms.

PHOTOGRAPHY: STEWART NIMMO

Greymouth

reymouth is the largest town in the West Coast region. Greymouth enjoys a collection of Art Deco buildings within an attractive compact town centre. Greymouth's coastal, river and bush-covered hill setting contributes enormously to the character of the town. The 1930s and 1940s buildings are well supported by the other commercial buildings of earlier and subsequent years.

The substantial Revingtons Hotel at 47 Tainui Street is a landmark building in Greymouth. A plain two-storey hotel frontage on the main road is in contrast to its Tainui Street elevation. Here it sets the standard for other two-storeyed buildings that make the Tainui streetscape, notably Waitaiki House and Hannah's Buildings.

Revingtons Hotel was constructed in 1938 and designed by Collins and Harman in the Spanish Mission style that was favoured in

hotel design in the early part of the twentieth century. The frontage contains a number of ornamental features and decorative ironwork.

The former National Bank of New Zealand at 102 Mackay Street is designed in the style adopted by the bank with the Stripped Classical elements and a decorated door pediment and parapet. The building was constructed in 1937. It currently operates as a photography studio and retail shop. The exterior has been modified by a glass canopy but the building is sympathetically presented and is a fine example of institution building of the time.

The Regent Theatre was officially opened on February 19, 1935. This large theatre on the corner of Herbert Street and MacKay Street was designed to host both live shows and the showing of movies and was considered a thoroughly modern theatre at the time. The building was designed by Llewellyn Williams

ABOVE: Revingtons Hotel in Tainui Street. The hotel hosted the Queen and the Duke of Edinburgh in 1953.

OPPOSITE PAGE: The National Bank of New Zealand was originally plastered with yellow sandstone-coloured concrete jointed out to give the appearance of blocks. The illustration shows the building in the late 1940s.

FROM THE TOP: The original Ford dealership in Greymouth operated from this building in the 1930s. Subsequent business, including a period as a Mobil service station and in 2016, for selling second hand goods; the Womens Centre at Guinness Street is a Centennial building in a characteristic Modern style.

and was part of the JC Williamson chain of picture theatres. It served a dual purpose with a live auditorium and has been used for both opera performance and movie showings. The cinema has assumed greater significance with the recent demolishment of the Avon Theatre in Christchurch, another William's design, following the Christchurch earthquake. It was built during 1933-1934 during the Depression and employed labourers. The backbreaking work on the new theatre was recalled with blood from blistered hands from the raw cement and unrelenting supervision. The decorative detailing of the interior of the building is largely intact with many of its original fittings and designs. Despite numerous modifications over the years, they have all been to the advantage of the building. The theatre occupies an ongoing part in the life of Greymouth. The exterior features some zigzag patterning as decoration.

The Women's Centre (1940) was a Centennial Project. It's design and modern appearance are typical of the small buildings erected in New Zealand during the celebration of the nation's 100 years mostly with the same style of lettering.

Built in the early 1930s the former Grey Ford Storage building is representative of a 1930s service station and dealership. It has gone through several changes in ownership including a period as a Mobil service stations. With no canopy from the elements, the building's functional purpose is relieved by layered columns on its front façade.

LEFT: Becks at 27 MacKay Street was an institution in Greymouth and served as a grocery, remodeled in the 20s, it retains today an intact shop frontage with leadlight and tiling.

BELOW: A contemporary illustration of the Regent Theatre.

PHOTOGRAPHY: VAUGH BRADLEY

Hokitika

ABOVE: The Regent Theatre in Hokitika and the building adjacent gave a distinctive Moderne look to the town centre in the 1950s.

The attractive Regent Theatre in the West Coast town of Hokitika is a notable surviving Streamline Moderne influenced theatre. The Regent bears a superficial appearance to the demolished Christchurch Avon Theatre (1934). The architect for the Hokitika theatre was Mr W Melville Lawry from Christchurch. Lawry had designed the West Avon apartments (1930). He also designed the Methodist Orphanage and Children's Home (1934) and Century Theatre (1940) in Saint Albans that have since been demolished.

HOKITIKA MUSEUM WESTLAND DISTICT COUNCIL

The privately owned Hokitika Theatre was completed in December 1935 with the opening held on January 10, 1936. It was an impressive building with a façade that radiates the excitement of the modern. It was a catalyst for the style adopted by other buildings in close vicinity. Directly across Weld Street was the long established Hotel Westland. This had been redesigned in mid-1930s with a distinctive modern parapet with parallel lines and similarly complemented both the theatre.

On the corner to the west of the theatre, the former W Perry and Co building was remodelled in 1951. This two-storey ferro-concrete building complemented the new theatre with a Streamline style façade topped with illuminated signage. The Regent part of town looked quite modern at the time. Adjacent commercial buildings designed in a Moderne style are uncommon in New Zealand and the former W Perry and Co Building has been remodelled with what remains of the original façade behind steel sheeting.

Other buildings include a Stripped Classical former National Bank on the corner of Hamilton and 46 Revell Street which was built in 1939. It shows some simple Art Deco elements including cornice fluting and a frieze of repeated overlapping half circles.

BELOW: The Hotel Westland circa 1950s on Weld Street.

Christchurch

A persistent symbol of the Art Deco era was the rising sun and the idea of the new dawn. It was a symbol used on New Zealand's most well-known building and gardens in the mid-twentieth Century – the Christchurch factory of Mr. Thomas Edmonds (1858-1932). Thomas Edmonds established a company to produce baking powder tins in the early 1900s. The Factory was built between 1920-1923. The architects were brothers, Mr. JS and MJ Guthrie from Christchurch and William Henry Williamson was the builder, who also built the Avon Theatre.

The cookbook printed by the company could be found in most New Zealand homes, the cover showing the factory and gardens and a decorative façade, a rising sun with the assurance in large type, SURE TO RISE. The three-storeyed Christchurch building was built with a saw-tooth roof to permit maximum sunlight, which was in accordance with Mr. Edmonds health philosophy. Thomas Edmonds was a philanthropist and a benefactor to Christchurch's civic architecture. He was also an enthusiastic gardener, and in accordance with the Garden City Movement, held the idea that the model factory should be beautiful for the benefit of its employees and the community. The iconic building and gardens were lost in October 1990 with the demolishing of the old factory and the removal of the gardens immediately in front of the building.

In the 1930s a new theatre opening was a real event: "From the swing doors at the wide entrance it is 22 feet across – a rich carpet slopes gently up past the two ticket boxes,

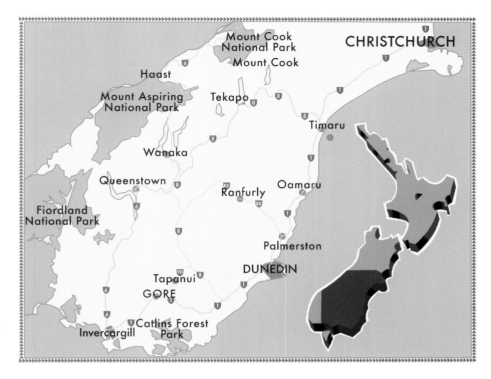

through the French-polished doors and into the large vestibule. Off this vestibule offices, and cloak rooms open. On either side easy flights of stairs with fascinating chromium-plated balustrades lead one to the spacious upstairs lounge, with its inviting chairs and settees, with more well appointed cloakrooms attached. The general colour scheme of the foyer is of varied autumn tints with here and there splashes of brighter colour.[1]

There were many Art Deco theatres in Christchurch. The most majestic was the five-storey Majestic Theatre (1930) built for John Fuller and Sons, with the Spanish Mission Radiant Hall, that later became the Repertory Theatre. There was also the Tivoli, originally designed by Wilford in 1934, the Avon (1935), the modernist State Theatre (1935) and the Century in Edgeware Road which opened on February 1940.

OPPOSITE PAGE: Edmonds Factory and gardens were probably the most well-known building in New Zealand in the mid-twentieth century being depicted on the cover of the best-selling Edmonds cookbook.

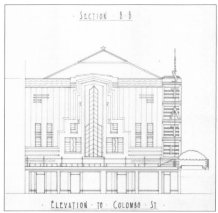

- SECTION - B-B -

- ELEVATION - TO - COLOMBO - ST -

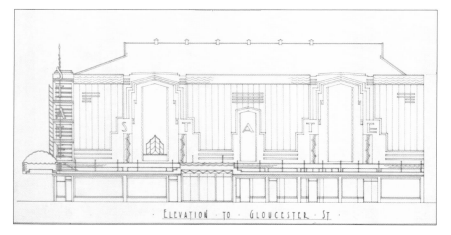

- ELEVATION - TO - GLOUCESTER - ST -

ABOVE: The façade for the State theatre as it was initially described at the time appears to have been finished in coloured cement (Cementone) in a terracotta with green and chromes. Following the fire in 1938, the State Theatre building interior was rebuilt and redecorated. Probably the smoke damaged exterior was painted over. Later images in the 1960s show the State Theatre exterior as being an all over grey colour. A glimpse at the colour under the cladding can be seen above. The illustration is based on the original plans and description of the appearance of the State Theatre in 1935.

Redesigning theatres to meet modern tastes was not uncommon in New Zealand. The Tivoli was originally Everybody's Theatre opened in 1915. It was redesigned by Cecil Wood in 1934 with input from Paul Pascoe to become the Moderne looking Tivoli Theatre.

The *Sun* newspaper recounting the opening, commented on the mirrors and chrome. The pale brown and turquoise interiors, and the staircase decorated by signs of the zodiac. In 1971 it became known as the Westend Theatre before closing down in 1994. The theatre was purchased by property developer David Henderson in 2003 and the old Tivoli façade was restored. In 2007 it was decided the site required demolition and the building was demolished in May 2007.

The Avon Theatre on Worcester Street was designed by architect Llewellyn Williams and opened in May, 1935. This theatre was designed in a modern style with parallel curvilinear incisions a projecting vertical windows and remained a popular theatre until the 1990s. The interior design was considered a major selling point of a theatre. The interior decoration of the Avon was described as being in the best modern style. The fan designs on the walls in bas relief were picked out in lighting. The reporter for the press on May 14, 1935 accounting the new facility writes in detail on the oyster gray walls with contrasting browns and ceiling design entirely hand painted in lasting pigments and confirms the eclectic nature of Art Deco theatres by noting that the zigzag motif is Norman in origin and others were Egyptian in origin.

The former State Theatre (1935) on the corner of Colombo Street and Gloucster Street was commissioned by Amalgamat-

ABOVE: The Avon Theatre as in late 1988. The illustration is based on an image from an unidentified newspaper cutting. The film showing, however, *Deathwish 4* starring Charles Bronson, provides a definite time period for this demolished and much-loved Christchurch Theatre.

RIGHT: The now demolished former Christchurch Repertory Theatre was originally known as The Radiant Hall and was founded by Christchurch benefactor and baking powder magnate, Thomas Edmonds. The illustration shows the original façade with glass canopy which was a treatment popular with building entrances during the 1920s.

BELOW: The Tivoli Theatre Christchurch (demolished) with a brightly painted Modernist façade as it appeared after restoration in 2004.

Dunedin

Art Deco buildings in Dunedin are uncommon but there is an abundance of magnificent buildings dating from Victorian through to contemporary. However the Art Deco examples the Otago city possesses are significant. These include the best example of a Streamline transport hub in the former New Zealand Road and Rail Services building at 35 Queens Gardens. The design looks to

the famous Streamline greyhound buildings designed in the United States by architect WS Arrasmith and conforms New Zealand's interest in that style in the late 1930s.

The architect was Eric Miller who worked with Edmund Anscombe, a distant relative, on the New Zealand and South Seas Exhibition of (1926). This important Art Deco building originally served the bus

ABOVE: The New Zealand Road and Rail services building, now the Otago Early Settlers Museum, is New Zealand's best Streamline transport building. Illustrated here as in the mid-1950s.

transport needs of the New Zealand Road and Rail services with its proximity to the Dunedin Rail Station an important consideration. As roads improved in the 1930s and bus use increased, there was a need to garage the burgeoning bus fleet as well as accommodate staff and provide cover for freight and passengers. With a Historic Places Category 1, the New Zealand Railways Road Services building now serves as the Otago Early Settlers Museum and has retained parts of the original interior.

Eric Miller as Messrs Miller and White also designed the ornate Otakou Māori Methodist Church was constructed during New Zealand's Centennial year. Located on Tamatea Road on the Otago Peninsula, the building has a fine site in rural countryside. The cost of the building was met by a government grant, the Methodist Church and local fundraising efforts. It was officially opened on March 22 1941. If one of the characteristic philosophies of Art Deco was to integrate indigenous designs and patterns into contemporary structures, then the Otakou Methodist Church is the most overt representation of this. The unique example of architecture features representations of traditional Māori carving de-

sign created in cast concrete. The design attempts to reconcile the principle structures of Māori wharenui with the spaces and layout associated with a traditional church. The repeat casting of the concrete decorative panels in the same moulds resulted in the decoration and building having an asymmetrical, conflicted appearance. The exotic church building for all its shortcomings, presents an entirely different engagement with Māori motif and art. Rather than the more assimilative treatment exhibited in Stripped Classical buildings, Otakou Church makes explicit the indigenous building styles. The leadlight windows in three colours only, are based on weaving patterns and the chancel was panelled with tukutuku panels. As an example of a definably 'New Zealand' Art Deco building Otakou Māori Methodist church has no equivalents. The adjacent Tamatea meeting house of Ngai-Tahu remains the other principle building on the site.

Although Art Deco nightclubs are synonymous with the Jazz Age, prohibition of New Zealand's social activities of the time centred around the town hall or hotels. The Crawford Lounge, in Dunedin's Crawford Street, was built in 1939 and was not a decadent speakeasy and had no liquor li-

PHOTOGRAPHY: SALLY KERR, STREET.JOHN, EILEEN STEPHEN, STREET.JOHN

THIS PAGE: Different views of the impressive Order of Street. John's buildings in York Place.

OPPOSITE PAGE: The Otakou Māori Methodist Church.

cence. The Crawford Lounge had a modern detailed façade. Advertising of the period exhorted potential patrons with the line: 'You've done the Lambeth Walk, now try the Crawford Lounge'.

The building still exists today although the Art Deco façade has been altered by a window addition. It is rare as a genuine surviving Art Deco club from the 1930s.

The Order of Street John at 17 York Place has been in Street John ownership since the mid 1930s. The two Art Deco buildings were built in 1937. The original buildings were the result of a considerable donation by Samuel Saltzman. The buildings were completed in 1938. The decorative plaster work is among the best in New Zealand and the whole conforms to what is obviously a well-con-

ceived building. The decorative frieze work is particularly notable. The Building is listed as a Heritage Category 1 building. The architects for the building were Dunedin architects Eric Miller and James White.

A new building to house the Ambulance Station was built in 1992. The architect for the 1992 buildings was McCoy & Watson. The new building replaced the 1956 Ambulance Station that had previously replaced the 1937 Ambulance garages. The 1937 buildings had alterations in the period 1955-1980, and an extension to the rear of the 1937 building was added in 1992. The entire complex is a very good example of building design where the additions have been highly sympathetic to an existing heritage building.

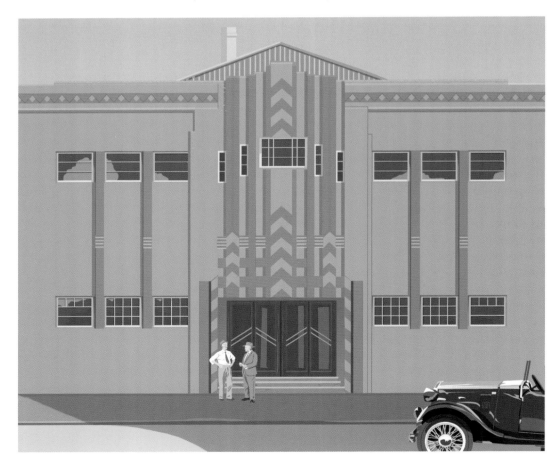

GLEN HAZELTON

Tapanui

PHOTOGRAPHY: JIM CREIGHTON

The small town of Tapanui has one of the oldest continuously running garages in New Zealand, with its overall appearance dating from 1938. Wylies Garage Ltd was established by 'Father' Wylie in 1922 and was built around the old Tapanui Presbyterian church, the brickwork of which is still visible at the rear of the building. The building has been modified and the present façade built in 1938. Other undated modifications have taken place and the building's evolution has taken it through over ninety years of motoring history.

In 1954 the garage had eight pumps: a Europa pump, a BP, two Caltex, two Shell

and two Mobil. During its existence the garage has been a New Zealand Road and Rail Depot, operated the school bus, delivered newspapers, operated taxis and leased rental cars. Today it still operates, performing an essential role in Tapanui and in the wider district providing fuel and vehicle servicing.

Gore

ABOVE: The view down Gore's 30s precinct Irk Street, the end of the former Latty's garage can be seen on the left.

The most obvious building in the Southland town of Gore is the five-storey historic Creamoata Oat Mill built in 1919 by a former family business established by Thomas Fleming (1848-1930). Fleming Co were producers of New Zealand's popular breakfast food, the milled Creamoata porridge for nearly a century. Fleming also milled flour and built mills in Dunedin, Winton and Mataura. Gores's Art Deco buildings were established in the company of a town with already a rich collection of historic structures. The Gore Town Hall fire in 1959, and the loss of all records including property files, has made it difficult to date buildings.

Gore's Irk Street is the heart of Gore's Art Deco street. The former Latty's garage and service station, originally designed in Streamline style complemented the Longford house building with its distinctive Moderne structure. The latter building design may well have been influenced by Anscombe's Centennial Exhibition in Wellington in 1940. In New Zealand terms the buildings on the street give us a rare glimpse of uninterrupted collection of Moderne style buildings.

The former garage, established by Mr Denis Latty both repaired and sold Ford motorcars. The dealership also sold petrol and the entire operation was designed in a distinctive modern style. The most striking feature is its two-level semi-circular tower and the strong curved end double lines of framing around the garage doors. The enigmatic spiral concrete post contributes to an almost sculptural whole. Although the modern-looking pump canopy is gone and the petrol bowsers have

been removed, the garage recalls an earlier period in motoring and design. Longford House (early 1940s) shares this modernity. The vertical decorative structures of the roof parapet, and the curved corner and the large block letters, announce the name of a rare style of surviving Streamline commercial building. More conservative are the buildings which share the curvilinear styling and modern inflections associated with the mid -1930s. These are Cranmer Court, the most substantial, with Farry's building being the last of the five.

On the eastern side of 61 Irk Street the SBS Street James Theatre constructed in (1936) is a modern restrained theatre. The horizontal incisions on the two-storey building, the simply fluted pilasters, and its modern appearance complements the buildings on the

TOP & ABOVE: Latty's garage depicted as it was in early 1960s with its Streamlined features, presenting a very modern appearance, and as it appears today.

TOP LEFT: Irk Street. Cranmer House dates from 1935 and the group of five buildings on the left date from the 1930s. With a number of undated Art Deco buildings due to the loss of records in 1959, Gore's Art Deco heritage is very apparent but more difficult to measure.

TOP RIGHT: A small two-storey modern style building in Gore's main street.

ABOVE & LEFT: Investment House and the La Hoods Chemist building, both appear in every respect to be 1930s buildings. Their position relative to the buildings in Irk Street provides Gore with an unique Art Deco presence.

most attractive buildings. Located at 65 Tyne Street, the building (1905) contributes to the variety of beautiful churches that are part of Invercargill's character.

From the outset, the intention of the congregation of the Central Methodist church in Invercargill in the 1930s was to embrace modernity in their design. The former Invercargill's Central Methodist Church located at 82 Jed Street was in conspicuous proximity to the ornate First Church. The Southland Times reported in April 1935 that the 'new church under construction was said to be a very modern one. In October 1935 the new church on the corner of Spey and Jed Street is described as 'essentially modern rather than elaborate in appearance. In fact the whole effect of the design is one of chase beauty.' A view no doubt aimed as much at the dazzling First Church which was three blocks further down the street as the readership. Modernity was to mark the Methodist church as it featured curved pews and a modern sound system to enable parishioners who were hard of hearing to partake of the service. The architect was Mr Edward H Smith.

There is little doubt the Church saw its new church in comparison to the Presbyterian First Church, which was the elaborate design of Invercargill's famous son, John Mair, who was at the time Government architect. It was designed to have a specific architectural relationship with the First Church and both possess the similar occupation of corner site, general layouts and dimensions. The Central Methodist Church's design in appearance features conspicuous stepped pilasters and cross integrated into the unmistakably modern tower. The design and angles of the brick tower, the angled coping and the

attractive stepped concrete entrance contribute to one of New Zealand's most remarkable Art Deco buildings.

Deco churches are rare in New Zealand. The Great Depression and World War Two contributed to this as much as conservative tastes in building. Hasting's Wesley Methodist church (1932) is an exception. The Napier Cathedral completed in 1950 and the Anglican churches at Levin, Palmerston North and Wairoa in the 1960s, often called 'Art Deco Churches', owe more to international style than the 1930s. Excluding Hasting's church (1932) (which was essentially revivalist in design) the former Central Methodist church in Invercargill represents New Zealand's only modern Art Deco church from the 1930s.

Contemporary examples of Art Deco vary in results. A notable exception is the Bill Richardson Transport Museum in Invercargill. This world-class collection of trucks cars and other vehicles is housed in a Streamline Moderne building constructed in 2015. The concept of Bill Richardson's daughter, Jocelyn O'Donnell, the inspiration came from the Art Deco style homes in Invercargill in the area. The resulting building façade, constructed by Calder Stewart Industries Ltd of Invercargill, is a contemporary representation of the Streamline style so identified with transport. The Museum's collection started in 1967 when Bill acquired his first vehicle and with thousands of artefacts, including around 300 vehicles, the museum establishes a significant Art Deco presence in Invercargill.

The design reflects the association of the style with the motor and transport industry internationally and also in New Zealand. While the building is not historic in itself, it is the most appropriate style of structure for housing an outstanding collection of vehicles many of which were operating during the 1930s through to the 1950s.

In the suburbs of Invercargill Art Deco houses continue to be prized homes and new generations of New Zealanders grow up in them and identify with Art Deco styling.

The Southland city of Invercargill, like most towns and cities has a typically small number of Art Deco buildings. However placed in a national context there is the opportunity to recognise the significance of individual buildings and the role they play in the history of the nation. Nationally the 1930s Stripped Classical post offices are the real cornerstone of New Zealand's Art Deco built heritage. Along with the 1940 Centennial Exhibition and associated buildings, they were designed to represent New Zealand's status as a modern nation, the whole being greater than the sum of its parts.

BELOW: The Bill Richardson Transport Museum in Invercargill, was originally established by the late Bill Richardson, an avid truck and vehicle enthusiast. The museum at 491 Tay Steet brings Art Deco élan in an eye-catching, streamline style of building.

Glossary

Art Deco A general term for the predominant decorative style of the 1920s and 30s mainly as architecture and domestic objects. The style first appeared in France and only became widely known after the 1925 *Exposition des Arts Decoratifs et Industriels* in Paris. In architectural terms it broadly covers: Stripped Classical, Spanish Mission, Streamlined Moderne, Moderne, and Art Deco itself.

Architrave Used to describe the vertical members of a frame or moulding around a door or window. It is frequently used to describe the style of mouldings framing the top of a door, window or other rectangular opening.

Californian Bungalow A popular style of house between 1910 to 1939. These are single or one and a half storey dwellings and typically feature a dormer window or attic vent, a partial-width front porch and are horizontal and in keeping with local materials and plantings.

Campanario The Bell Tower usually on a Spanish Mission building.

Campanile A bell tower that is generally free standing.

Capital This is the topmost element of a column and frequently decorated with botanical subjects. In Art Deco Stripped Classical buildings, the capital was often simplified.

Chamfer An edge or corner that has been cut off diagonally.

Chicago School Was a group of architects and engineers who, in the late 19th century, developed the skyscraper. They included Daniel Burnham, William Le Baron Jenney, John Root and the firm of Dankmar Adler and Louis Sullivan.

Corbel A projection, more usually a series of projections, supporting an overhanging element.

Cordova Tile A curved, terracotta-coloured tile used extensively in Spanish Mission style.

Dentil Moulding This is the repeated small block ornamentation in a cornice. It is not usually associated with Art Deco but was most evident in Georgian style buildings built in New Zealand.

Fanlight A small window opening over a larger window.

International style A major architectural style that emerged in the 1920s and 30s. The emphasis was on architectural style, form and aesthetics rather than the social aspects of the modern movement as emphasised in Europe. Characterised by rectilinear forms, taunt planes stripped of ornamentation, open interior spaces. Glass and steel were the predominant materials of this style.

Koruru This is the figure in Māori building placed at the apex of the gable of a whare.

Oriel Window A window that projects from an upper storey, supported by brackets or corbelling.

Parapet A low wall on the roof, balcony or terrace.

Pediment This is the non-structural element seen over windows and doors. In Art Deco styles, this element is most apparent in Spanish Mission buildings.

Pilaster Pilasters have the appearance of a flattened, low profile column. Pilasters can have a plain or fluted appearance. The element is common in Stripped Classical style buildings that were constructed in New Zealand in the 1920s and 1930s.

Spandrel On multi-storeyed buildings, this is the panel, often sculptured, between the top of the window on one-storey and the sill of the window in the storey above.

Spanish Mission Architecture that originated in the south-western States of America, and had the characteristic of smooth cream walls, which echoed the lime washed plaster mud brick walls of the early Catholic Spanish Missions. The parapets were often tiled in terracotta to protect the walls from erosion and rain. Windows could be large and arched or small and square with other decorative elements like inlaid tiles, and wrought iron.

Stripped Classical A modern stripped down version of Classical architecture that dates from the Edwardian era. Classical details were reduced in number and became less imposing. Columns were flattened and ornamentation more restrained, often only on the capitals and parapet.

Vestibule An entrance hall, lobby or antechamber.

Ziggurat These massive structures were built in the ancient Mesopotamian valley and western Iranian plateau, having the form of a terraced step pyramid of successively receding stories or levels.

Acknowledgements

Aden Shillito, Nick Paris, Lisa Manhire, Bill McKay, Erin Kimber, Max Podstolski, Chris Coster, Scott Bond, Peter Wimsett, Mercedes Waitere, Glen Hazelton, David Murray, Lorraine Johnston, Anna Peterson, Eileen Stephen, Ian Henderson, Shirley Kerr, Jackie Dobson, Christine Page, Bruce Cavanagh, David Luoni, Alan Ritchie, Margaret Phillips, Jim Geddes, Vince Latty, Jim Creighton, Margaret Mort, Stewart Nimmo, Chris T. Johnson, Perry Rice, Nikki Roche, Lynn Millar, Sue Asplin, Vaughan Bradley, Julie Grut, Wendy Adlam, Clark Stiles, Rebecca Smith, Graeme Williams, Catherine Skerrett, Sally McDonald, Kaaren Metcalfe, Bruce Ferguson, Nicola Smith, Noma Shepherd, Dionne Ward, Gareth Winter, Adam Simpson, Dr Ann McEwan, Paul Harrington, Stephen Rainbow, Nan Owen, Dianne Brody, Linley Davies, Bruce Lea, Gerry Parker, Gilda McKnight, Heather Glasgow, Chris Rollitt, Diane Paterson, Petra Zoe, Annemieke Dabb, Gregg Brown, Stephen Cook, Ron Cooke, Rodney Giddens, Stephanie Smith, Clare Street. Pierre, Haylee Alderson, Jim O'Halloran, Jean Hitchen, Althea Barker, De Alison, Michael Draper, Dionne Ward, Tiena Jordan, Viv Hynds, Pearl Edwards, Richard Overy, Gillian Tasker, Simon Bloor, Sandi Black, Ian Lochhead, Win Matthews, Sarah File, Nikki Newton-Cross, Robbie Walker, Nicola Zaaiman, Rosie Ellis, Sharlene Tornquist, Alex Cowie, Lori Adkins, Bill Brown, Rose Jackson, Leyton Chan, Lisa Truttman, Liz Clark, Harold Hancox, Jocelyn O'Donnell, Colin Prince, Michael Fowler, Sally Jackson, David Gibson. Special thanks also to the children of Kaiwaka Primary School, Henry Mancini, Monkey the cat, Paula the dog.

Photography
Dionne Ward, Stewart Nimmo, Trefor Ward, Gerry Parker, Alan Ritchie, Jim Creighton, Jackie Dobson, Bruce Ferguson, Heather Glasgow, Clare Street Pierre, Julie Grut, Glenyss O'Halloran, Denise Skilton, Charles Richard Bruning, Mercedes Waitere, Matt Wiseman, Stephen Rainbow, Rodney Giddens, Petra Zoe, Paul Harrington, Adam Simpson, Tim Whittaker, Gregg Brown, Simon Burt, Johan Rijnbende, Eileen Stephen, Shirley Kerr, Jack Moyle, Terry Moyle.

Notes

Introduction

1 Renwick, W, *Creating a National Spirit: Celebrating New Zealand's Centennial*, Victoria University Press, 2004. p50.
2 The New Zealand Yearbook 1940.
3 New Post Office New Zealand Herald, Volume LXXVII, Issue 23829, 3 December 1940.

Napier

1 Shaw, Peter, *A History of New Zealand Architecture* p127.
2 *Railway Magazine*, November 1935.

Auckland

1 King, Jenifer, Sign of Service: A Jubilee History of the Auckland Electric Power Board, 1922-1972.
2 Shaw, Peter, Ibid. p136 .
3 From Modern Design *Auckland Star*, Volume LXXIV, Issue 212, 7 September 1943.
4 Advertisement for Hotel Titirangi, JT Diamond Collection, West Auckland Research Centre, Waitakere Central Library, JTD-10A-01675.

Warkworth

1 Rodney, Waitamata Times and Kaipara Gazette, 29 September 1937, p9.

Hamilton

1 New Post Office, New Zealand Herald, Ibid.

Wellington

1 *Auckland Star*, May 1, 1940, p4.
2 Shaw, Peter, ibid, p137.

Christchurch

1 *Modern Theatre Press*, Volume LXXI, Issue 21499, 14 June 1935.
2 Plea to restore Old Theatre, *The Press*, 30 November, 2011.